Contents

ATTILA
King of the Huns

CHAPTER ONE

Barbarians Invade Europe

THE STING of a gadfly is said to have started a mass migra-
tion of fierce barbarians into Europe. Cities in the path of
the invaders were turned into ashes and people put to the
sword. During the first half of the fifth century A.D., savage
Huns threatened to destroy Christianity and the civilized
world.

At the height of the Huns' barbaric rule in Europe, one
man reigned over an empire extending from China westward
to the Atlantic Ocean. He was Attila the Hun, whose name
has come down through fifteen hundred years of history as
a symbol of ferocity.

According to the gadfly legend, recorded in the historical literature of the fourth and fifth centuries, the Huns and the Goths lived side by side for many years without either knowing of the existence of the other. The two nations were separated by Kerch Strait, a narrow, shallow waterway between the Sea of Azov and the Black Sea. The Huns roamed the wilderness east of the strait in the region known today as the Georgian Soviet Socialist Republic. The Goths inhabited the peninsula of Crimea. The peoples of both nations, thinking the world to be flat, believed that there was no land over the horizon.

The legend told by ancient Roman, Gothic, and Greek historians says that one day a heifer which belonged to the Huns was stung by a gadfly, a large, winged insect that feeds on horses and cattle. The heifer fled across the marshy waters of Kerch Strait to the opposite shore, into the land of the Goths. The herdsman plunged into the water and followed the animal. He struggled through the mud and marsh until he, too, reached the opposite shore.

Weeks later, the herdsman returned. He told his fellow Huns of the mild climate and the fertile soil of the Crimea. It was a land of plenty. The Huns, always in great need of food, their lives spent mostly in the cold reaches from the Caspian Sea north to the "frozen ocean," lost no time in seeking out this land of plenty. Hordes of hungry Hunnish tribesmen crossed Kerch Strait, conquered the Goths, and began their ravishing onslaught of western Europe.

The Huns reached the peak of their power in Europe in the twenty-year period between A.D. 433 and 453 under Attila, king of the Huns.

CHAPTER TWO

Origin of the Huns

THE BABY ATTILA was snatched from his mother's arms only minutes after his birth. His father Mundzuk, king of the Huns, stood by as a weird and brutal ceremony was performed. One Hunnish warrior held the wailing baby in his arms. Another warrior slashed the infant's cheeks with a sword. The baby, his face bleeding, was handed back to his mother.

The Huns believed that each male child must be taught to endure a wound before being permitted to receive nourishing milk from his mother. The early pain would make him a bold and ferocious warrior—if he survived. Attila, despite his royal birth, was no exception.

Just where and when this strange ceremony took place is not known. One historian says that Attila was born in a chariot as his family's tribe roamed the plains of Hungary near the Danube River, then called the Danubius, in A.D. 395. However, it is more generally believed today that Attila was born about A.D. 406 in an encampment on the Danube in Hungary, near the site of the present-day city of Budapest.

Whatever the actual date of Attila's birth, the Huns had left the eastern shores of the Sea of Azov, crossed the marshes of Kerch Strait, and had begun their ravages of western Europe long before Attila came into the world. The conquests of the Huns, the total destruction of all that they conquered, and their ferocity first came to the attention of the powerful Roman Empire about A.D. 375.

The Roman historian Ammianus Marcellinus, who died in A.D. 398, wrote of the Huns: "They are faithless in truces and they burn with an infinite greed for gold." All historians agree that the Huns lived like wild beasts. It was regular practice for them not only to kill off the old men of their tribes but to eat their bodies.

The ferocity of the Huns struck terror into the people of the areas which they devastated. The invaders would strike like lightning, swooping down on their fast horses, howling madly, lashing out with long, black, snakelike whips, and dragging lariated victims behind them as they rode away. Then they would disappear as quickly as they had come. As the populace of the area regained its breath, believing it had been spared, the Huns would return. This time they would cut down the shocked population with sword and spear, bow and arrow, completing the devastation that they had started before.

Word spread quickly when the Huns began to ravage an area. The frightened people became even more horrified when they got their first look at the barbarians. The Huns conquered as much by their hideous appearance as by their might.

The Byzantine historian Priscus wrote of the Huns: ". . . they put to flight by the terror of their looks, inspiring [their enemy] with no little horror by their awful aspect and by their horribly swarthy appearance. They have a sort of shapeless lump, if I may say so, not a face, and pinholes rather than eyes. Their wild appearance gives evidence of the hardihood of their spirits, for they are cruel, even to their children on the first day they are born. They cut the cheeks of the males with a sword so that before they receive the nourishment of milk they are compelled to endure a wound. They grow old without beards, and the youths are without good looks, because a face furrowed by a sword spoils by its scars the natural grace of a beard. Somewhat short in stature, they are trained to quick bodily movement and are very alert in horsemanship and ready with bow and arrow; they have broad shoulders, thickset necks, and are always erect and proud. These men, in short, live in the form of humans but with the savagery of beasts."

The Huns increased their ugliness by deforming their skulls during childhood. Flat boards were placed on either side of the head, and the boards were drawn together by leather thongs, elongating the head, and pointing it at front and rear. Adding to their savage appearance was the clothing which the Huns wore—smelly skins of wild beasts and fur headgear. Their only footwear was wide cords of leather.

The animalistic traits of the Huns extended to the food they ate. Mares' milk was their drink and raw meat their food. The raw meat was made tender by carrying it between the thighs of the horsemen and the flanks of their horses. Attila never tasted any form of bread in his whole life.

The Huns were so ugly that they were regarded as the offspring of fiends and witches. Attila was a true Hun, his appearance definitely stamping his origin. "He exhibited the genuine deformity of a modern Kalmuck (Mongol)," wrote a Gothic historian. "He had a large head, a swarthy complexion, small, deep-seated eyes, a flat nose, a few hairs in place of a beard, broad shoulders, and a short, square body of nervous strength though of a disproportioned form. The haughty step and demeanor of the king of the Huns expressed the consciousness of his superiority above the rest of mankind, and he had the custom of fiercely rolling his eyes as if he wished to enjoy the terror which he inspired."

Where the Huns originally came from and where they lived in the era before their invasion of Europe is disputed by ancient Roman and Greek historians. Only fragments of their writings have been preserved.

Ammianus described the origin of the Huns: "The nation of Huns, scarcely known to ancient documents, dwelt beyond the Maeotic marshes beside the frozen ocean, and surpassed every extreme of ferocity."

Priscus, who once visited the camp of Attila as an emissary

of the Roman Empire, had a different version of how the Huns discovered and invaded Europe. His story is somewhat like the gadfly legend but seems more realistic because it fits the Huns' habits.

"Their cruel tribe," Priscus wrote, "settled on the farther bank of the swamp of Maeotis. They were skilled in hunting but in no other task except this. After they had grown into a nation, they disturbed the peace of neighboring races by thefts and plundering.

"While the hunters of this tribe were, as usual, seeking game on the far bank of Lake Maeotis, they saw a deer appear unexpectedly before them and enter the swamp, leading them on as a guide of the way, now advancing and now standing still. The hunters followed it on foot and crossed the Maeotic swamp, which they had thought was as impassable as the sea. When the unknown Scythian land appeared, the deer disappeared. (The Crimean Peninsula was part of Scythia.) The Huns, who had been completely ignorant that any other world existed beyond the Maeotic swamp, were filled with admiration of the Scythian country, and, since they were quick of mind, believed that passage, familiar to no previous age, had been shown to them by the gods. They returned to their own people, told them what had happened, praised Scythia, and persuaded them to follow along the way which the deer, as their guide, had shown them."

Before coming to the shores of the Caspian and Black seas, the Huns may have lived in nomadic tribes on the high plateaus of Central Asia. As far back as 200 B.C., according to one theory, the Huns ranged and terrified all of Asia,

7

from the Volga River eastward to the Pacific Ocean. They warred constantly with the Chinese and extracted heavy tributes from them. The Chinese areas which the Huns conquered were stripped of food, and the Chinese were forced to pay large sums of gold to the Huns each year. The Huns also forced the Chinese to release their fairest maidens to become the wives of Hunnish chieftains.

A Chinese verse, which has lasted through the ages, tells the sad song of a Chinese princess who was forced to become the wife of a Hun chief. She moans of her sad lot, forced to drink sour milk as her only liquid and to eat raw flesh as her only food. Her palace was a tent, and she spent her days wishing she were a bird that she might fly away.

Modern ethnologists, experts on the origins of cultures and races, identify the Huns with the Mongolian people of northern Asia who invaded the Chinese Empire around 200 B.C.

Wherever they came from, whatever time they appeared, the Huns brought to history a man who would be called "the Scourge of God"—Attila the Hun.

CHAPTER THREE

Attila Grows Up

UNTIL HE WAS ABLE to walk, Attila's home was the chariot which followed his father's tribe on its raids for food and gold. The Huns were on the move most of the time, abandoning an area after they had plundered it to strike out for another. Rarely did they remain in one place for more than a few weeks. Not until Attila was a young boy did the Huns build their wood-enclosed tent village along the Danube.

As soon as Attila was able to toddle about on his short, stumpy legs, his training as a warrior began. When the future king and other Hun children his age were still too young to ride on horses, they were mounted on sheep. Their pudgy hands grasped the sheeps' wool as older boys sent the animals careering about the plains and through the woods. Soon the young leg muscles grew firm. Attila could sit astride a sheep and not be thrown off, no matter how wildly the sheep might run and swerve. Then a small bow and some arrows were placed in his hands. Now the real training began. Hour after hour, mounted on his woolly charger, Atilla practiced killing rabbits, birds, and other small game.

Lessons in the use of the sword, the spear, the lariat, and the whip came next. When his legs were sturdy enough to grip the flanks of a horse, Attila gave up his sheep for the larger animal, and was given bigger weapons to handle. He soon became skilled in the use of these tools of war and hunting, and took part in many raids on small villages, riding alongside his father, King Mundzuk.

One historian wrote that none of Attila's boyhood associates was as expert at throwing the lariat, cracking the whip, drawing the bow, and handling the lance as was the future king of the Huns. Attila soon began living, eating, and even sleeping, while astride his horse.

When a village had been conquered by the raiding Huns and the fighting was over for a time, the restless Attila would take to the hunt—riding down deer, killing wolves with his bow and arrow, or running them through with his spear. Larger game, such as bears, were first captured by hurling a huge net over them. Then the young hunters, led by Attila, would slaughter the beasts by cutting them open with short daggers.

During Attila's boyhood, the Hun capital was wherever the huge encampment of skin-covered chariots happened to be stopped. The chariots were the homes of the Hunnish

10

families, and they accompanied the warriors on their almost continuous migrations. The warriors rode ahead; the women and children followed in their chariots.

The Huns fought not only for food but for gold. They were the first mercenaries of recorded history. (A mercenary is a soldier who serves only for pay or gain.) Like later mercenaries, they did not care about the cause of the war and so they fought on any side. On some occasions, Hunnish tribes fought in the pay of the Roman Empire. At other times, they fought as paid members of the enemies of Rome. The Hun nation was made up of numerous tribes, each tribe maintaining its own independence. Sometimes the tribes would unite against a common enemy; sometimes one tribe of Huns might fight against a brother tribe, if there was gold to be won.

To try to keep its paid Hunnish allies in line, Rome instituted the practice of exchanging members of Roman nobility for young princes of Hun chieftains. In actuality, the young Huns were hostages. When Attila was twelve years old, he was sent to the court of Rome as one of these hostages.

On the death of Attila's father, King Mundzuk, Attila and his elder brother Bleda became wards of their uncles Rugila, Oktar, and Aebarse. Supposedly, Attila was the favorite of Rugila, but the uncle lost no time in getting rid of his young nephew who was already beginning to show signs of independence. Attila was particularly opposed to the practice of the Huns hiring themselves out as warriors for other nations. Rugila, who had often committed his tribe to fight with the Roman legions, sent young Attila to the court of Flavius Honorius, ruler of the Western Roman Empire.

Attila hated his life in Rome. Accustomed to the freedom

11

of hunting and fighting on the plains along the Danube, he was like a caged animal in the palace where he was virtually a prisoner. The delicate and elaborate food dishes of the imperial household were rejected by young Attila, who preferred his diet of raw meat and mares' milk. He was surly and never hid his anger or dislike of his Roman hosts. The Romans added to Attila's hatred by making fun of the ugly, ill-mannered youth.

Attila made several attempts to escape. Each time, guards caught him and brought him back. There is no record of how long he spent at the Roman court, or how he was finally returned to the Hun capital on the Danube. But return he did—full of anger and hatred for the Romans.

Attila's experiences at the court of Rome did much to formulate his plans for the future. His deepened hatred of the Romans caused him to dream of one day ruling the world. He would unite the Hunnish tribes. Never again would a Hun serve in the army of an enemy, particularly in the service of the Romans. Attila would one day destroy the Roman Empire. All these dreams and ambitions burned in his mind. For the present, however, Rugila was king of the largest Hunnish tribe, and Attila made no attempt to seize control from him.

Little is known of Attila's young manhood. It is believed that he traveled widely in Europe and Asia. He hunted, took many wives, and waited for the death of his uncles. During the years before he came to power, he carefully made his plans. His day would come. With Asiatic patience, he awaited that time. The day came nearer with the death of Oktar, who was killed while leading his tribe against the

Burgundians in western Europe. Aebarse was having his troubles with the unruly barbarians of the Caucasus. Of the three ruling brothers of the Huns, Rugila reigned over the most powerful group and was threatening the Roman Empire of the East.

Attila followed closely every move his uncle made; he would be ready to take over when Rugila fell.

CHAPTER FOUR

King Attila

THE GREAT Roman Empire began to decline in the first quarter of the fifth century. On the death of Theodosius I, in A.D. 395, the Empire was split in two. One son, Flavius Honorius, became emperor of the West with his court at Rome. Theodosius' other son, Arcadius, became emperor of the East with his court at Constantinople.

Rome had been attacked three times by Alaric, king of the Visigoths, who finally captured the city in A.D. 410. But Alaric moved on and settled in Gaul, and Honorius regained rule of the Western Empire. In 425, Valentinian III became emperor of the West, but he was a weak prince and his mother, Galla Placidia, actually ruled for him.

15

Theodosius II succeeded Arcadius in A.D. 408 as the emperor in Constantinople. Attila's uncle Rugila extended his rule over Slavic and Germanic tribes and was now important enough to receive a yearly tribute of three hundred and fifty pounds of gold from the Eastern emperor.

This was the setting when Rugila died and Attila became king of the Huns in A.D. 433. Although Attila's elder brother Bleda shared the rule with him, Bleda's authority was in name only. He was weak and did not dispute his younger brother's right to supreme authority.

When news of Rugila's death reached the Byzantine court of Theodosius II in Constantinople, the Roman Senate decided to send emissaries to the new rulers of the Huns. Plinthas and Epigenes, two court officials, were chosen as envoys to the Hunnish court. Their mission was to extract better terms from the new rulers than those which had been negotiated by Rugila. After all, the new Hun leaders were young, and Plinthas and Epigenes were veterans in dealing with enemies of the Byzantine court.

At this time, Attila was in camp near the mouth of the Morava River, not too far from what is now the city of Dubrovnik in Yugoslavia. Plinthas and Epigenes, weary from their months-long ride on horseback from Constantinople, entered the camp of the Hun king to receive a totally unexpected reception. News of the emissaries' approach had been brought to Attila by guards stationed at outposts. When the Roman envoys rode up, they were not even allowed to dismount. They were informed that the king awaited them, and a group of horsemen was pointed out to them. In the group were Attila, Bleda, and their aides.

16

The king of the Huns sat motionless upon his horse. He was dressed in a short, black fur jacket. A black fur cap was pulled down low over his eyes. Beside Attila, Bleda, a giant in size compared to his brother, stared down at the envoys. Plinthas and Epigenes were informed that they would not be permitted to dismount. Negotiations would be carried on while the participants sat on their horses. This reception dismayed and angered the envoys of the imperial court of Theodosius II. They had expected a warm reception from Attila, believing that his stay in Rome as a youth had acquainted him with some of the court etiquette.

Plinthas began to speak. Before he had completed a sentence of his formal opening of greetings, Attila interrupted him with a gesture that silenced the envoy. Bleda, although senior in the joint kingship, uttered not a word.

Attila spoke. He wasted no words. He stated the conditions under which the Huns and the Byzantine Empire could remain at peace. They were not conditions; they were demands.

The Roman envoys had no chance to present the terms which Theodosius II had empowered them to offer to the new king of the Huns. Attila, whom they had expected to be more reasonable than his predecessor Rugila, was just the opposite. He spoke in a hard voice. He was arrogant— even contemptuous—of the envoys of the Byzantine court. He brushed aside every attempt of the Romans to interrupt as he set forth his demands.

The Roman Empire in Constantinople must immediately stop all support to the barbarian tribes along the Danube who were resisting the Huns, Attila told them. All Hun

17

deserters, now in Roman territory, must be returned. All Roman prisoners who had escaped should also be returned, or the equivalent of eight pieces of gold per prisoner must be paid to the Huns. Emperor Theodosius himself must swear an oath never to give any assistance to enemies of the Hunnish empire.

Plinthas and Epigenes were shocked by the severity of the demands laid down by Attila. As they began to gasp their shocked protests, Attila staggered them with the most extreme demand of all. The tribute which the court of Theodosius was now paying to the Huns must be doubled; increased from three hundred and fifty pounds of gold yearly to seven hundred pounds.

The Roman envoys tried to persuade Attila to discuss the demands which he had laid down. Attila was immovable. There would be no discussion, he said. The Romans asked for time to consider the demands. Attila's reply was that he wanted an answer at once.

"What is the alternative?" the Roman envoys asked.

Attila's reply sent a chill through the two Romans. The alternative was war!

Quickly the envoys agreed to the return of Hun deserters. They would also return escaped Roman prisoners, since eight pieces of gold per head was too costly. They agreed that no longer would the Byzantine Empire aid the barbarian enemies of Attila. They would also try to persuade Theodosius to promise not to wage war against the Huns. This reply came easily from the mouth of Plinthas. He knew that Theodosius was in no position to war on the Huns. The Byzantine Empire was too weak to do so. When it became strong again, such a promise could readily be broken.

But the last of Attila's demands brought the strongest protest. The Roman Empire of the East was nearly bankrupt. More taxes to increase the yearly tribute to seven hundred pounds of gold was out of the question.

During the protest by Plinthas and Epigenes, Attila remained silent. The two envoys might well have shouted their protests at a mountaintop.

Attila repeated his earlier statement—peace or war? Which would it be?

The envoys capitulated. They agreed to every demand. The Treaty of Margus, which was then the name of the Morava River, was signed, and Plinthas and Epigenes turned their horses back in the direction of Constantinople, dreading the tale they would have to bring to the emperor.

The terms of this treaty were lived up to by Theodosius II. Among the Huns returned under Attila's demand were two children, Mama and Atakam, scions of one of the Hunnish royal houses. They had been taken along by their parents when Attila subjugated the tribe and brought it into his armies. The children were crucified as a penalty for the flight of their family, and as a warning to other Huns against desertion.

Attila, victor without a struggle in his first test as king, now turned his attention to unifying the numerous Hunnish tribes into one great nation of Huns.

CHAPTER FIVE

A Bold Move

THE TASK which Attila had set for himself was a gigantic one. But so was the Hun king's goal. He burned with a driving ambition to one day rule the world. He would conquer Europe. Then, rich with the treasures plundered from Rome and Constantinople, he would hurl his hungry hordes on Asia, crush Persia, India, and China. The last country to feel the might of the Huns would be Africa. Genseric (also called Gaiseric), king of the Vandals who ruled Africa, would be driven from his throne. Attila, king of the Huns, would then be king of the world, ruling over all the lands from the China Sea to the Atlantic Ocean.

It was a bold dream that raced through Attila's head. The plan would stagger a less ambitious man. But Attila, though short in stature, was big in desire and full of confidence, never doubting that his grand plan could be anything but successful.

First, however, Attila must rule all the Hunnish tribes. He must subjugate the Asiatic branches of the Huns and bring all tribes from the Danube to the Volga under one leader—himself.

Never in the history of the Huns had they been firmly united under a single leadership. They were not so much a nation as a network of hundreds of small tribes, held together only by their language and traditions. These tribes —some numbering not more than eight or ten families, others numbering thousands of members—led the here-today-gone-tomorrow lives of nomads. Each tribe was an autonomous group, its king governing as he wished. The king led his tribe into pillaging for his own and for his tribe's benefit. Once a region had been devastated, its resources exhausted, the tribe was on the move again. No one knew, or cared, what the destination might be, so long as the new home would provide the meager daily needs.

As king of the Huns in the Danube region, Attila had no authority over the Huns in Asia or Russia. So he set out to change all this, and he did.

The Treaty of Margus was not only Attila's first victory, it was a steppingstone to his greater goal. The Roman envoys Plinthas and Epigenes had been most alarmed by Attila's demand for a yearly tribute of seven hundred pounds of gold. In this one point, Attila had shown his superior diplomatic skill over the veterans of the Byzantine court. The demand for seven hundred pounds of gold was actually a smoke screen. More important, although lightly regarded by the emissaries of Theodosius, was the demand that the Roman Empire cease giving any support to the enemies of the Huns. Attila's plan was to conquer, with little or no opposition, all the smaller nations standing between him and his goal. A second highly significant point in the treaty was the demand that all Huns who had deserted or who were in the pay of the Roman Empire be returned.

Although these two points seemed of little consequence to the Roman rulers, there was one man who understood their significance. He was the Roman general, Flavius Aëtius. Aëtius had long and loyally served the court of the ruler. He was a skillful general, a shrewd diplomat, a man of great foresight. During his many years of service, at times Aëtius had been a hero to the Romans, at other times an outcast removed from power by little more than the whim of the court, or by an ambitious seeker of his position. Aëtius had been banished by the court on several occasions, only to be brought back to power when the safety of Rome was threatened.

This Roman general, who was born about the same time as Attila and, like him, had been a hostage in Rome as a youth, had followed Attila's moves closely. He alone read the true meaning of the Treaty of Margus. He saw how Attila had increased his power by enslaving the peoples of the lesser nations in the Danube Valley. Aëtius knew that the most serious threat of all Attila's demands was the one which required the Roman Empire to send back to the

23

Hunnish nation all deserters and Hun warriors serving with the Roman legions. It was clear to Aëtius that Attila no longer intended to permit any Hun to serve as a soldier of a foreign power. Attila was determined not only to unify his people but also to deprive the Roman Empire of its best fighting men. The men who had been fighting for the Romans would now be added to Attila's swelling army and would become the foes of their former employers.

Although Aëtius saw through Attila's plans, even he did not realize the full scope of the Hun king's ambition.

Attila, with the barbaric enemies of the Danube under his control, and fearing no immediate threat from either the Eastern or Western Roman empires, turned his attention to the Caucasus, where his last surviving uncle, Aebarse, ruled the Caucasian Huns.

Under the laws of royal succession, Aebarse should have become king of the Huns when Rugila died. But Aebarse was far removed from the Danube and satisfied with his own rule over the Caucasian Huns. When he learned of his brother's death, he made no move to establish his right to rule.

Aëtius, seeing a chance to frustrate Attila's plans, tried to bring about a split between Attila and Aebarse. He sent envoys to Aebarse's camp. The envoys pointed out to the Caucasian Hun ruler that his nephews had usurped his rightful throne. They wanted not only to alarm Aebarse, but to make him jealous of his youthful nephews. Aebarse's own throne would be endangered if he allowed Attila and his brother Bleda to continue the plan for unifying the Huns.

Aebarse was easily convinced. He sent messengers to the

Hun capital on the Danube. They were instructed to inform Attila and Bleda that Aebarse would permit the young kings to remain in power, but that he would never give up his authority over the Caucasian Huns. In taking this position, Aebarse detached himself and his subjects from the Hun nation, making the Caucasian Huns completely autonomous.

In this skillful move, Aëtius had help from Emperor Theodosius. The ruler in Constantinople sent representatives to the many independent tribes roaming the plains along the Don River, arousing in them a fear that they would lose their freedom if Attila were allowed to carry out his plans for unification.

One of these Hun tribes was the Akatziri, a fierce and highly independent group. It was a large tribe with many chieftains. Attila learned that the Akatziri chieftains had received rich bribes from the Byzantine court to revolt against Aebarse as a step to establish their complete independence and to continue their revolt against Attila.

Attila might never have learned of the Byzantine bribes had not the Romans made a mistake. It would prove to be a most costly one. In handing out the bribes, the Roman envoys, for some unexplainable reason, overlooked an old chieftain called Kurdiak. Perhaps because of his age, the bribers felt that Kurdiak could be bypassed. But they did not take into account the old man's pride. Despite his years, he remained well up in the hierarchy of authority among the chieftains. Other Akatziri chieftains received handsome Roman bribes. Kurdiak received none—and he was angry. He felt that the Romans were trying to undermine his position among the chieftains. So Kurdiak informed on his colleagues and on the Roman ambassadors who had failed to send him jewels, silks, and money. He sent messengers to Attila informing him of the plot.

Attila took immediate action. He realized that if the Romans were allowed to continue their subversive activities, his plans to bring the Caucasian Huns under his rule might become most difficult to carry out. Attila gave his brother Bleda the authority to handle affairs along the Danube, and he left at once to confront his uncle Aebarse.

Aebarse had not seen his nephew for many years, but Attila's reputation for cruelty, daring, and ambition had preceded him. Aebarse dreaded the upcoming meeting. He was old, and not too secure in his rule with the Akatziri threatening open rebellion.

Much to Aebarse's surprise, Attila's first greetings were most friendly. But as their conversation progressed, Aebarse became alarmed. In Attila, he saw a young man of strong will, a man determined to achieve his goal. Attila outlined his plan for world conquest to the older man. He said that almost all of the Hunnish nation was under his control. He explained that it was only natural to encounter some resistance, but to overcome this resistance would take no more than a single command. None of the tribes had been able to resist thus far; none could resist him. Sensing that Aebarse was weakening to the point of capitulation, Attila assured Aebarse that he knew he could count on his uncle's complete cooperation. He also hinted that Aebarse would regret it if he preferred to act otherwise.

Aebarse gave in. He declared himself in complete support of his young nephew. As further proof of his loyalty to

Attila's cause, Aebarse turned over a large number of his most fierce horse-borne warriors to swell the army that had accompanied Attila.

The problems with Aebarse disposed of, Attila directed his next move against the revolting Akatziri tribe. He would not be able to deal so easily with them. Attila had withheld any punishment from his uncle for his threatened revolt. But with the fierce Akatziri, he would have to deal more harshly.

Once again, Kurdiak came to Attila's aid, although this time indirectly. When the Akatziri heard that Attila was descending upon them, they prepared for war. Kurdiak, fearing that his fellow chieftains might learn that he had warned Attila of the plot against him, took a large number of his warriors and fled to the mountains, many miles away from where the clash between Attila and the Akatziri chieftains would take place. Greatly weakened by the loss of Kurdiak's large force, the Akatziri were easily overcome. Attila severely punished the leaders of the Akatziri, executing many of them. But since he wanted the loyalty of the rank and file warriors, he did not punish them and, instead, extended to them a welcome to join his forces. This invitation was readily accepted.

Attila wished to thank Kurdiak for his help. He dispatched a messenger to Kurdiak's mountain hideout, inviting the leader to join him. Kurdiak's reply was that he was an old and tired man, adding that his eyes, too weak to look upon the sun, were certainly too weak to behold the brilliance of Attila the conqueror. Attila accepted this flattery for what it was worth. He knew that the principal reason for

Kurdiak's refusal was the old man's fear of reprisal from his conquered fellow chieftains.

To make sure of his ruling position among the Akatziri, Attila placed his eldest son Ellak on the Akatziri throne as their king. Ellak had instructions to keep a close eye on all moves made by his great-uncle King Aebarse.

Attila moved farther into central Asia. Everywhere he went he conquered. Tribe after tribe was added to his growing nation. He raided and conquered along the shores of the Baltic Sea. Although his journey took several years, he felt that the time was well spent for he added hundreds of thousands of Hunnish tribesmen to his cause.

It was now time for Attila to return to the Danube. No word had come to him of any great unrest. The Roman empires had not attacked, nor did they threaten. It seemed that all was well in the vast region that he had left for so many years. But Attila was wrong. His brother Bleda, made bold by his long rule as sole king along the Danube, had let his power go to his head.

CHAPTER SIX

The Sword of Mars

ATTILA WAS FURIOUS with his brother, for Bleda had become arrogant. He had enjoyed being the sole ruler of the Danubian Huns during his brother's years-long absence. He had entertained ambassadors. He had made treaties—minor ones, but he had made them. Having become accustomed to power, he wanted to keep his position. He did not want to be a king in name only as he once had been.

Bleda was unable to conceal his shocked surprise when Attila rode into the Hun capital on the Danube. He had long felt certain that Attila must have been killed during the many years he had been away. Now his dream of sole rule was shattered. Bleda proposed to Attila that they share more equally in their joint kingship. Bleda would turn back to Attila part of the duties of the joint monarchy. Attila listened to his brother, apparently agreeing with him. But Attila was laying his plans. Something would have to be done about Bleda, and Attila lost no time in doing it.

A few days after Attila's return to the capital, he suggested that he and Bleda go on a hunting trip. Bleda willingly agreed, feeling that he had convinced Attila that they share in the rule of the Hunnish nation. The hunting party returned three days later with Bleda's body borne by members of the party. He had been killed in a hunting accident.

Rumor swept through the Hunnish capital. Attila had killed his brother. Members of the hunting party were silent, and Attila did not even deny the whispered charge. Bleda was dead. Attila was the sole ruler of the Huns. That was the important thing. It was never actually proven that Attila murdered his brother, but all historians agree that this had to be the case. It was in character with Attila. He would allow nothing or no one to stand between him and his goal.

For a short time after the murder of Bleda, there were murmurs of discontent in the Hun capital. What manner of man was this who would murder his brother? But those who might have started a revolt against Attila were soon silenced. An event took place, attributed to the supernatural, that forever put a stop to questions of Attila's divine right to sole rule.

A herdsman tending cattle on a plain outside the capital noticed that one of his heifers was bleeding badly from one hoof. What could have caused the deep cut? Curious, the herdsman followed the path of bood until he came to a thick clump of grass. He parted the grass and saw the point of an ancient sword sticking upward. The herdsman's curiosity was heightened. This could not be a sword dropped in the heat of battle. Its hilt was buried in the ground. Eagerly the herdsman pulled out the sword and hurried to Attila.

The sword was proclaimed as the sword of the king of the Hun dynasty. It had been handed personally to the king by Mars, the god of war. The sword of Mars had been lost for hundreds, even thousands, of years. The legend was that the sword would be discovered during the reign of the true and rightful king of the Huns. Possession of the sword of Mars was indisputable proof of its owner's divine right to rule the world.

Attila took quick advantage of this miraculous find. It was a gift of the gods, he proclaimed, and a great ceremony must be made to celebrate the gift. A lofty altar was erected on a broad plain outside the capital. It was three hundred yards in length and breadth. At the summit of the altar, the sword of Mars was placed. Consecration services began by drenching the altar with the blood of sheep and horses. Then the hundredth prisoner was counted, and his arm and shoulder cut off. These were thrown high on the altar, and from the manner in which they fell, priests and soothsayers read their omens.

The sword of Mars was brought down from the top of the altar and placed in Attila's right hand. A torch was put to the altar. Attila stood immobile as the altar burned to the ground.

No longer could anyone question Attila's right to the

throne. He was king of the Huns, wielder of the sword of Mars, long reserved for his invincible arm. He would rule the world.

Those who had cried out against Attila's murder of his brother were silenced forever. The murder, said the superstitious Huns, had been dictated by the gods. The sword of Mars was the proof.

Shortly after this event, Attila received another startling gift. He and the Huns interpreted this gift as a second sign that destiny favored the ambitions of the would-be ruler of the world.

A messenger named Hyacinthus from the Western court in Rome rode breathlessly into Attila's camp along the Danube. He demanded to see the king of the Huns. Questioned by guards and minor Hunnish officials, the messenger insisted that he could speak only with Attila. He had risked his life in his mad dash from Rome. He had outwitted Roman soldiers sent to intercept him. His message was for the king's eyes alone.

It was a strange and startling message which the Roman delivered to Attila—a letter from the Princess Justa Grata Honoria, daughter of Galla Placidia and sister of the Roman Emperor Valentinian III. Honoria had sent her ring to Attila to secure his aid against her brother.

Attila interpreted the ring as an offer of marriage. But this was shocking—unheard of! A royal princess of the great court of Rome was beseeching a barbarian to marry her. It was a puzzling offer, although a flattering one, and Attila suspected a trap. But after further questioning of the courier, Attila learned of Honoria's motives.

Strong-willed and ambitious, Honoria despised her weak brother, Valentinian. She had become involved in the intrigues of the court. But Valentinian suspected that Honoria and the manager of her affairs were plotting against him, so he had his sister's manager put to death. He then ordered Honoria to marry Flavius Cassius Herculanus, an older man of consular rank, and highly regarded for his loyalty to the court of Rome. As her husband, Herculanus would be expected to curb Honoria's ambitious plans, which included her dream of succeeding her brother to the throne. (However, fifteen years were to pass before Honoria and Herculanus would be married.)

Honoria also offered Attila a large sum of gold to save her from Valentinian. With Attila's help she would get her revenge against her brother.

Attila carefully considered Honoria's strange proposal. A union between a royal princess and a barbarian king could be of great advantage to Attila. But he also saw the disadvantages. He felt certain that Valentinian and his brother Theodosius would wage war on the Hun nation if Honoria managed to slip out of the Roman court and make her way to Attila's camp. Attila was not ready for war with the Roman Empire. When he was ready, he would wage war at his own instigation.

Honoria's plea was ignored. Attila would wait and learn of the outcome of Honoria's apparent folly. He sent Hyacinthus back to Rome without a reply, but the messenger was captured before he could reach Honoria. He was tortured by Valentinian and revealed Honoria's plot. Hyacinthus was beheaded, and Honoria was handed over to her mother

33

Galla Placidia, who had her locked up in a convent in Ravenna.

Attila kept the ring. He did not try it on, since he well knew of the practice by ruling monarchs of sending poisoned rings to their enemies. The ring and the letter were placed in a small casket. At some time the ring and letter might be of value in Attila's long-range plans against the Roman Empire.

CHAPTER SEVEN

Gold for Attila

THE TIME was approaching when Attila would make his first move toward his goal of world conquest. The Hun ruler carefully reviewed the positions of his enemies.

The Chinese presented no threat at the moment. Peaceful relations between the Huns and the Chinese had continued ever since Attila's long expedition into Asia. He had reached the Great Wall of China. He had met with Chinese rulers and had made peaceful overtures. The Chinese, also wanting peace, had made agreements with Attila. In the years since his visits, Attila was careful to send ambassadors to the Chinese courts. Lavish gifts were exchanged regularly. One day

Attila would smash the Great Wall and conquer China. For the present though, the Roman Empire must be brought to heel.

Attila knew that the Roman Empire in the West was plagued with troubles. Valentinian sat uneasily on his throne. The Vandal King Genseric was reducing Rome's last holdings in Africa to ashes. Sicily had been attacked; Carthage had been captured and lay in ruins. For a long time, Africa had been the source of grain for the Romans, and a complete cutoff of this grain was a serious threat.

Valentinian summoned Aëtius and instructed him to build a large fleet for an attack on the king of the Vandals. But carrying out this royal order was another major problem. The Roman treasury was nearly bankrupt. Besides, Aëtius could no longer count on hiring Hunnish mercenaries to wage his wars. Attila had seen to this. Romans would have to make up the legions of warriors, and the Romans, used to hiring others to do battle for them, had little liking for the proposal that they themselves now take up arms.

For these reasons, Attila felt certain that the Roman Empire in the West presented no immediate threat. He was further assured since there had been no repercussions resulting from Honoria's request.

The Roman Empire in the East, ruled by Theodosius II, was already paying tribute to the Hun nation. The Treaty of Margus had given Attila a free hand in subjugating those barbaric tribes which were his enemies.

The problem that faced Attila was where to strike first. Should the Roman Empire in the West feel the full onslaught of the Hunnish hordes, or should he attack the East?

But before Attila could strike at any court, he first had to solve another major problem—money. A great war chest of gold would be needed to carry out a full-scale attack against the Roman Empire. It was true that Attila ruled a large nation, and that the Huns occupied and controlled vast territories. But these territories supplied only the immediate needs of the many Hunnish tribes. They did not supply gold in sufficient quantities to fill Attila's war chest.

Over a period of years, Attila had received a supply of gold through trickery from the two Roman empires. He had sent ambassadors to the courts at Constantinople and Rome who promised to betray Attila. Bribery was a common practice among all courts, and in return for the false promises the Romans filled the pockets of the Hunnish ambassadors with gold. On returning to the Hun capital on the Danube, the ambassadors poured the gold into Attila's war chest.

Attila took great enjoyment from tricking the Romans. One day he would use this Roman money against those who were handing it out. However, the "bribery" money was a mere trickle. Attila needed gold in much larger quantities. He decided that the Roman Empire in the East would be his best source of the much needed money. He would start a series of harassments against the Byzantine court of Theodosius II, arousing in them the fear of an all-out attack. Then Attila would make his demands for gold.

The first strike by Attila's hordes came against the city of Margus. Fierce horsemen raided the city during its annual fair. The ruthless Huns swept through the marketplace, cutting down merchants, burning, and pillaging. Hundreds were killed. Theodosius protested that Attila had violated the

Treaty of Margus. Attila replied that his raid was made to revenge the spirits of former Hunnish chieftains. Their graves had been despoiled by the Roman Bishop of Margus when he had searched for the treasure chests of the former Hunnish chieftains.

Attila did not stop there. He demanded that Theodosius surrender the Bishop of Margus so that he might be properly punished for desecrating the graves. The Bishop, knowing that this punishment meant death, surrendered the city to Attila.

With Margus under complete Hunnish control, Attila led his loot-hungry tribesmen to the city of Naissus near the Morava River, today the city of Niš in Yugoslavia. Naissus was the birthplace of Constantine, one of the greatest of all Roman emperors. The city was fortified, surrounded by a high wooden wall. Within this circular wall, machines of war were made. Attila wanted the city. He wanted to capture the craftsmen and their war machines.

But Naissus presented a new problem to Attila and his army. The Huns were accustomed to fighting on open plains. They had little experience in attacking a walled and fortified city.

Attila, riding at the head of his army, called a halt one hundred feet in front of the high walls. He ordered his troops to surround the city, and his horsemen dashed into position. The wall was soon encircled by fierce riders, their spears ready.

A shout to surrender came from Attila's lips. The shout was picked up by the Hunnish warriors, and the cry ringed the city. But the reply came quickly as a rain of arrows shot down from the wall top. Attila's men returned the fire. Bone-tipped arrows flew back, bounding off the wall and causing no damage. A second flight of arrows came from the defenders of the city. Many of Attila's men and horses were cut down. Attila ordered his men to draw back out of range.

A council of war was held. Taunts and insults were shouted at the defenders in an attempt to bring them outside the walled city to fight in the open, but the defenders refused to leave.

The Huns now brought their machines of war into position. These were huge battering rams, copies of those used by the Roman legions, and Attila had seen them in use. Many of his Hunnish warriors had used them when serving as mercenaries in the pay of the Romans. The Huns would now turn them against the Roman enemy.

The rams were large wooden beams mounted on wheels for easy movement. Hunnish soldiers stood atop the wooden beams, firing arrows at the battlements as the rams were brought into position. The warriors on the beams wore protective garments made of rawhide interwoven with twigs, and leather shields to ward off the hail of arrows fired at them from atop the battlements.

The huge wooden beams were rolled into position at the foot of the wall. Soldiers furiously began to get the battering rams ready for operation. Protected by their rawhide clothing, they raised two huge timbers over each ram. These timbers were inclined toward one another until their tops met, forming an inverted V over the battering rams. Chains were dropped from the top of the V and fastened to the battering ram below. The cart carrying the ram was removed.

Now the ram was ready, swinging freely from the timbers supporting it.

The battering rams had huge metal heads. Warriors seized the ropes attached to the rear of each ram, and hauled backward. At a shouted command, they released the ropes. The ram swung forward in a deadly arc, smashing against the wooden wall. Atop the walls, the defenders of the city hurled down huge stones by the wagonload. The stones had been gathered as the rams were being brought into position. Many of the rams were destroyed and the men manning them crushed to death. But there were too many rams and too many Huns.

Gaping holes were smashed in the walls. The Huns, now shouting and grinning ferociously, rushed through the gaping wounds in the wall and hurled themselves on the defenders with sword and spear.

Other Hunnish warriors threw rope-scaling ladders to the top of the wall. They scrambled up, leaping down among the swarming battlers to join them in hand-to-hand combat. Soon it was all over and the city was captured. Attila rode through the breeched wall. The city of Naissus was his.

Theodosius II, alarmed by the fall of Margus and further frightened by the capture of Naissus, ordered his legions to defend other towns in the Huns' destructive path. But nothing could hold Attila back. Seventy more towns fell to his army. When Attila reached the Pass of Thermopylae, Theodosius sent emissaries to ask for a truce.

Attilla agreed, but Theodosius was made to pay dearly for the peace he sought. There was to be an immediate payment of six thousand pounds of gold. The yearly tribute from the

Byzantine court must be tripled—raised from seven hundred pounds of gold to twenty-one hundred pounds. Twelve pieces of gold must now be paid for the return of every Roman prisoner instead of the former head charge of eight pieces.

Theodosius agreed to these demands. He signed the treaty bringing the invasion to a halt. However, the harsh demands exacted of the Byzantine court at Constantinople resulted in a plot to assassinate Attila.

CHAPTER EIGHT

The Byzantine Court

ATTILA HAD BROUGHT Theodosius II to his knees. The Roman Empire of the East was nearly bankrupt. To raise the gold to meet Attila's demands, the Grand Eunuch Chrysaphius, Chief Sword-Bearer and Finance Minister to Theodosius, taxed everyone from millionaire to the poorest tradesman.

Theodosius, who lived in royal splendor, did not care about the welfare of his subjects. Chrysaphius, as the emperor's closest adviser, saw to that. He kept the palace bountifully supplied with every desire of the emperor. The populace could starve, but the Grand Eunuch was not going to jeopardize his position by having his emperor worry about how to meet Attila's demands.

Attila had a deep distrust of eunuchs. When he was a hostage at the court in Rome, he had seen how eunuchs regularly betrayed their masters, diverting collected funds into their own pockets. Attila felt that Chrysaphius would be no exception.

To ensure payment of the large amounts he had demanded, Attila dispatched two of his most trusted aides to the Byzantine court. Their purpose was threefold. They were to negotiate new boundaries between the Hun nation and the Byzantine Empire; closely watch Chrysaphius; and demand the return of Hun deserters who, Attila insisted, were still in the protective custody of the Romans.

The two aides chosen for this mission were Edeco, a Hun and Attila's chief bodyguard, and Orestes, an Illyrian from the land of Pannonia (now western Hungary). Orestes had defected to the camp of Attila. By a strange circumstance, Orestes was the father of Romulus Augustulus, "Little Augustus," who was to become the last emperor of the Roman Empire of the West.

Theodosius gave immediate audience to the two envoys of the Hun king. However, he was disdainful, even contemptuous, of Orestes, whom he considered a deserter and a traitor. He listened more closely to the words spoken by Edeco, a member of the Hunnish royalty. When the two envoys were dismissed, they were taken in hand by Bigalas, an interpreter and a high attaché of the Byzantine court. Bigalas informed them that they must present themselves to Chrysaphius. Orestes and Edeco went willingly, knowing that the Grand Eunuch was the power behind the throne.

As they passed through the vast hallways of the palace on their way to the apartments of the Grand Eunuch, Edeco the barbarian was overawed at the splendor confronting him. He had never visited a Roman palace before and was dazzled by its contrast to the wooden houses of the Hunnish camp. Edeco stopped again and again to marvel at the intricately designed vases that lined the hallways. He touched the rich brocaded tapestries. Beautiful marble sculptures caught his eye.

Bigalas closely observed Edeco's admiration for the luxurious settings of Roman royalty. Shortly after Orestes and Edeco had been presented to Chrysaphius, Bigalas held a whispered conference with the chief chamberlain. Chrysaphius listened carefully as Bigalas told him how Edeco was overwhelmed by what he had seen. A plot began to form in the mind of the Grand Eunuch.

After a brief audience with Chrysaphius, Orestes and Edeco were shown to their quarters. Edeco was placed in a high-ceilinged, luxurious suite to impress him further with the splendor surrounding high officials of the Byzantine court and its guests. Shortly afterward, Edeco and Orestes were surprised by a second visit from Bigalas. He brought them an invitation to dine with Chrysaphius that night. Edeco was highly pleased by this request, but Orestes was suspicious.

A sumptuous feast was served to the two envoys from Attila's court. Orestes had eaten such dishes before, but Edeco, whose life diet had been raw meat and mares' milk, was overcome by the delicacies served to him. On orders from the Grand Eunuch, servants kept Edeco's goblet filled with wine. Following the dinner, Chrysaphius personally conducted Edeco through his apartment. He showed the

Hun his official robes, heavily embroidered with gold leaf and precious stones. Chests of jewels were opened before Edeco's startled eyes. Silver and gold vases were everywhere. Heady with wine and gorged with rich foods, Edeco was fast becoming a witless tool in the hands of the smooth-talking Chrysaphius.

The two returned to the dining hall, and Chrysaphius, carefully drawing Edeco out, nodded his head toward Orestes and Bigalas. The two were engaged in serious conversation concerning the next meeting with the Byzantine emperor. Chrysaphius pointed out to Edeco that Orestes was apparently taking the lead in forming the strategy which would force Theodosius to yield to Attila's demands for new boundaries.

Chrysaphius played his hand skillfully. He stressed the fact that Orestes was not a Hun, although an adviser to Attila. He wondered out loud why Edeco, a member of Hunnish royalty, was obviously being treated by Orestes as an aide, rather than as an envoy of equal rank. Should not Edeco be the true representative of the king of the Huns? Chrysaphius had placed his opening wedge. If he could make Edeco jealous of Orestes, the chamberlain's path to his final proposal would be made smoother.

With a shrug of his shoulders, Chrysaphius seemed to dismiss the matter. Perhaps, he told Edeco, it was because Orestes was a man of great wealth. Great wealth, he continued, could bring a man the splendor of royal rooms in a golden-roofed palace. Edeco could become such a man. The dazzled Hun inquired how this sumptuous living could be attained. Perhaps it could happen, replied Chrysaphius, if

Edeco leaned more toward Roman ways and was less loyal to his king Attila. Did Edeco have easy and ready approach to his king? Edeco assured him that he did. He was intimate with Attila at all times. As his chief bodyguard, Edeco also directed the other guards who surrounded the king of the Huns.

Edeco tried to discover what Chrysaphius had in mind, but the Grand Eunuch felt that he had brought Edeco along far enough for that night. He directed Bigalas to escort the two envoys back to their quarters. As they were leaving, Chrysaphius whispered to Edeco that he would see him the next morning. Edeco was not to say anything of this to Orestes.

In the morning, Orestes was taken on an extensive tour of Constantinople, and Edeco was brought again to Chrysaphius' apartments. The Grand Eunuch questioned the Hun closely. He wanted to learn if Edeco, sobered by his night's rest, was still the naïve, wide-eyed barbarian, awed by a display of riches, as he had been the night before. He inquired again about Edeco's control of Attila's bodyguards. Edeco replied that as chief bodyguard he personally selected the guards to protect his master. Chrysaphius was satisfied. He offered Edeco his hand, and the two men swore oaths of secrecy about the proposal that Chrysaphius was about to make to Edeco. He exacted a promise from Edeco that should the Hun not wish to go along with the proposal, he would forever remain silent about it. Edeco agreed.

The Grand Eunuch asked the big question. On Edeco's return to Attila's camp, would he be willing to slay his master? With Attila removed, Chrysaphius hurried to explain, Edeco could come back to Constantinople. He would have a happy life and great wealth. Indeed, at this moment, Chrysaphius was ready to place fifty pounds of gold in Edeco's hands if the Hun would agree.

Hesitating only a moment, Edeco agreed.

Chrysaphius summoned a servant. The chamberlain had been so certain of Edeco that the servant came in bearing a bag containing fifty pounds of gold. The Grand Eunuch directed the servant to place the bag at Edeco's feet.

Surprisingly, Edeco refused the gold. The astonished Chrysaphius asked him why—and was delighted with Edeco's explanation. He was now even more certain that Edeco would carry out the plot to assassinate Attila.

Edeco explained that on his return Attila would question him closely about the gifts that he had received from the Byzantine court. Attila would be particularly interested in how much money he had received. This was always the king's first question to his ambassadors returning from foreign courts. Edeco also pointed out that it would be difficult for him to conceal from his companions a bag containing fifty pounds of gold on the long journey back to the Hun capital.

Edeco proposed a different plan for the delivery of the gold. He suggested that Bigalas return to the Hun camp with him and Orestes. Bigalas' function would be to give Theodosius' reply to the Hun's demands. This done, Bigalas would return to Constantinople, report to Theodosius, and come back to the Hun camp with the gold payment for the assassination. The killing would most certainly have taken place by then, Edeco assured the Grand Eunuch.

Chrysaphius was delighted with this plan. Bigalas would not only deliver the Byzantine court's reply to Attila but would serve as a watchdog on Edeco. Secretly, Chrysaphius hoped that Edeco and Bigalas would be found out as co-conspirators and both be put to death. That would eliminate the necessity of paying the fifty pounds of gold. It would also eliminate Bigalas, whom Chrysaphius had never liked, since Bigalas was an ambitious man.

With the plans arranged, Chrysaphius, in high spirits, asked for an audience with Theodosius. The Grand Eunuch laid his assassination scheme before his emperor. To the credit of Theodosius, the emperor at first refused to consider the fiendish plot.

But Chrysaphius worked on his emperor smoothly, slowly, persuasively. His clinching argument was that for the sum of fifty pounds of gold, the Byzantine Empire would be relieved of an economic drain that might bring it to bankruptcy. Fifty pounds of gold, Chrysaphius pointed out, was almost nothing compared to the yearly twenty-one-hundred pounds that Theodosius had agreed to pay the barbarian king. With Attila dead, almost all the problems of the Roman Empire would be ended.

Theodosius agreed. However, he ordered that the mission be headed by a Byzantine court member of unquestioned honesty. The man selected was Maximinus, who held a higher position in the court than Bigalas. Maximinus would present the statement of Theodosius' position on Attila's demands. He was to do this in a face-to-face meeting with Attila. Bigalas was to take orders from Maximinus and act only as an interpreter. However, Maximinus was not informed of the plot to assassinate Attila. Bigalas was also to do whatever Edeco thought best in arranging the final details of the assassination.

Another addition to the party was Priscus, a young scribe and historian noted for his cleverness and the elegance of his writings. He was to observe and record all the happenings that took place. Large fragments of Priscus' writings of this journey have come down through history and they give the best picture of Attila's court and the lives led by the Huns.

The following day, the party set out on the journey back to the land of the barbarians. Chrysaphius eagerly awaited the mission's return with the word that Attila, king of the Huns, was dead.

CHAPTER NINE

Attila's Camp

THE LONG JOURNEY from Constantinople to Attila's capital on the Danube took several weeks. The large party traveled in a single group, but divided into two groups for eating and sleeping. The Romans would not sleep in the same tents with the barbarians, and they were revolted by the raw meat and mares' milk.

After thirteen days, the group reached Sardica, now Sofia, in Bulgaria. The party had traveled as rapidly as it could, and it was decided to halt for the day and an overnight rest. Maximinus, Bigalas, and Priscus invited Edeco and Orestes and their servants to dine with them. Sheep and cattle were purchased from the local inhabitants, slaughtered, and prepared for the feast. During the meal, an incident took place that nearly brought on a brawling fight between the two groups. This quarrel was to be important when the mission reached Attila's camp.

Toasts were made. The barbarian envoys praised their leader Attila, and the Romans replied with toasts and praise for the Emperor Theodosius. Bigalas angered the barbarians by saying that it was not fitting to toast the two leaders at the same time. He said that it was wrong to compare a man with a god. He meant, of course, that Theodosius was the god and Attila but a man. The Huns resented this and, with angry shouts, drew their swords.

Maximinus and Priscus acted as peacemakers. They turned the talk to other matters and finally calmed down the excited Huns. Maximinus went even further. He hurried to his tent and came back with his arms filled with silken garments. These he presented as gifts to Orestes and Edeco, and threw in for good measure a handful of precious Indian pearls.

The day was saved and the barbarians were placated. Edeco soon retired, but Orestes remained behind. He told the Romans that he had been highly annoyed at not having been invited to the final banquet that Chrysaphius had given to Edeco. He knew that his conducted tour of Constantinople had been a ruse to get him out of the way. Then Orestes praised Maximinus. He hailed him as wise and noble. Maximinus had given no offense, he said, but others at the imperial court had. Edeco had been wined and dined and presented with fine gifts while he, Orestes, had been overlooked.

Neither Maximinus nor Priscus knew of the plot to assassinate Attila or that it had been hatched during the feast which Orestes referred. They questioned Orestes at length, but since he knew nothing of the assassination plot either, he had no explanation for what he considered shabby treatment. But he was very angry.

Priscus and Maximinus reported this conversation to Edeco as the party moved toward Attila's camp. The Hun had a ready explanation. He said that Orestes had no reason to be angry. Orestes was really only a servant and a secretary to Attila, but he, Edeco, was a man high in the military councils of the king. He was Attila's chief bodyguard and intimate friend. Furthermore, he pointed out, he was a member of Hunnish royalty and that alone made him far superior to Orestes. Priscus and Maximinus were satisfied with Edeco's explanation.

Several days later, the party reached Naissus, the fortified city that Attila had captured some months before. The Romans were shocked by the destruction. The city had been razed. There were no able-bodied men about. They found wounded men dying, women and children sick and starving. The Romans tried to set up their tents by the bank of the river, but it was impossible. Everywhere along the riverbank were strewn the bones of those slain in the battle. They had to establish their camp several hundred feet back from the water. Priscus, surveying the dreadful scene, wrote: "Where the Huns have passed, no grass will ever grow again."

The party finally reached the Danube where Attila had set up a temporary camp, hundreds of miles south of the Hun capital. Crossing the Danube, the barbarians escorted the Romans to within eight miles of Attila's headquarters.

Here the Romans were told to wait while Edeco and some of his party went on to herald the arrival of the envoys. Bigalas protested. He wanted to accompany Edeco and keep him under observation, but his protests went unheeded. Edeco departed, after having ordered several of his barbarians to remain as guards of the Romans.

The Roman mission waited all that night. Not until the following day, about 3:00 P.M., Priscus wrote, was the party brought to Attila's headquarters. The Romans began to pitch their tents on a nearby hill, but barbarian guards tore the tents down. They pointed to Attila's tent below. No one, they shouted, Roman or Hun, was allowed to dwell on a level above the great king of the Huns.

Several days went by before the embassy from Constantinople was received by Attila. The king of the Huns had sent word to Maximinus that he knew all the terms in the letters from Theodosius. Therefore, it was not necessary for him to waste his time in receiving the embassy.

This message worried Bigalas. He had not seen Edeco since the embassy had reached Attila's camp. Had Edeco revealed all to his master? Had he betrayed Bigalas and told Attila of the assassination plot?

Priscus and Maximinus, still unaware of the plot, thought that Attila's refusal to receive them might well be based on the incident that had taken place at Sardica. They suggested that Edeco might have told Attila that Bigalas had called the Roman emperor a god and Attila a mere man. If this had happened, Attila would be furious. While the three envoys were engaged in this discussion, they were suddenly summoned to appear before the king of the Huns.

54

When the Romans reached Attila's tent, they were stopped. A squad of guards surrounded them and then escorted them inside. They looked up at Attila, seated on a high, wooden chair. There was silence for several moments as Attila glared down on the Romans. Bigalas looked around, searching for Edeco. He saw him standing just behind Attila's makeshift throne, but Edeco refused to meet Bigalas' eyes.

Attila nodded his head, and Maximinus stepped forward. He bowed low before the barbarian king and handed him the letters from Emperor Theodosius, stating that the emperor prayed that Attila and his followers were safe and in good health.

Attila's reply was double-edged. "May it be unto the Romans as they would have it be unto me."

The king of the Huns took the letters from Maximinus but did not even glance at them. He turned his angry eyes on Bigalas, and denounced him as a "shameless beast." He angrily demanded the reasons for the mission from Constantinople. The terms of the Treaty of Margus were well known, he shouted. The Romans had not returned the fugitive Hun deserters. The Roman court had no right to send its ambassadors to the Hunnish court until all the fugitives had been surrendered to the barbarians.

Bigalas replied that there was not a single refugee of the Hunnish race among the Romans. All of them had been surrendered. This reply made Attila even angrier, and he screamed at Bigalas. Attila shouted that he had considered impaling Bigalas and giving his remains to the birds for food. He had not done so only because it was against the laws

55

of a diplomatic embassy to treat its ambassadors in such a fashion.

Attila ordered Bigalas to leave the camp at once. "Go back to Constantinople," he shouted, "and tell the emperor that all Hunnish refugees must be returned at once or war will result."

Bigalas was only too happy to comply with Attila's shouted order. The Roman felt now that Edeco had not revealed the assassination plot to his master. The order to return to Constantinople for fugitives was a scheme, perhaps planted in Attila's mind by Edeco, so that Bigalas could get the fifty pounds of gold. It would be handed over to Edeco when Bigalas returned to find that the king of the Huns was dead.

Maximinus and Priscus were commanded by Attila to remain with the Huns and make the journey with them to the Hun capital on the upper Danube.

It was again a long journey. Priscus, in his journal, described the many rivers crossed—the greatest of which was the Danube—before they came to the shores opposite the Hun capital.

As the party entered the capital with Attila in the lead, row after row of young girls greeted them with Hunnish songs in praise of the great king of the Huns. They walked in rows in front of Attila, with white linen cloths stretched over their heads. Each cloth was stretched so that seven to ten girls walked under one piece.

On a hill nearby, the Romans caught their first glance of Attila's palace. It was crude compared to the Byzantine palace in Constantinople, but it held beauty in its very simplicity. The palace had been built of highly polished timbers and boards. A wooden palisade encircled it, not—according to Priscus' journal—for safety but for beauty. Next to the king's dwelling was the house of Onegesius, second to Attila in power. This house, too, was outstanding and encircled with timbers. But it was not embellished with towers like Attila's.

When Attila rode up to the house of Onegesius, the wife of the second in command appeared, followed by many servants. The servants carried trays heavily laden with food and wine. Onegesius' wife pleaded with Attila to take food and drink. It was considered the highest of honors if Attila would eat with any of his barbarians.

Attila reined in his horse. Still astride, he took some of the food as it was handed up to him on a silver platter. He also sipped some wine. His stop was brief, a gesture to Onegesius. Then Attila rode to his palace on the highest ground in the city.

CHAPTER TEN

Attila's Banquet

WEEK FOLLOWED WEEK as Maximinus and Priscus remained in the Hun capital. The Romans were given freedom to roam through the sprawling village of chariots and tents. Many of the Huns, even though resting in the capital, still lived in their chariots. Only the wooden enclosure encircling Attila's quarters and those of his closest associates were denied to the Romans.

Priscus sent word to Attila that he had many presents for Attila's wife which he wished to present to her. Her name was Kreka, and she occupied the number one position of all the women in Attila's court. She had borne him three

59

sons, whom Attila had designated as his heirs. Attila also had about three hundred other wives. Many of them were in quarters in the capital, others lived in Hunnish villages throughout the nation.

Permission was granted to Priscus, and on the following day he entered the enclosure. Inside there were many fine wooden houses, all made of hand-carved curved planks, beautifully fitted together. The curved planks were laid on smoothly planed beams to form circles. The circles began at ground level and rose up in a series to considerable height.

Guards ushered Priscus into Kreka's private suite. He found her lying on a raised platform covered with soft, thick spreads of felted wool. Servants-in-waiting surrounded her, forming a large circle. At the foot of her platform, maid-servants sat on the floor, embroidering fine linens with colored threads. These linens were used as ornamental outer garments worn over the barbarian's rough clothing of animal hides.

There was no conversation between Priscus and Kreka. He formally presented his gifts and withdrew.

Not long after this, toward the end of the Romans' stay in the Hunnish capital, Priscus and Maximinus were invited by Attila to attend a banquet which was to begin at about 3:00 P.M.

On the threshold of Attila's banquet hall, the Romans were met by cupbearers. They had been informed in advance of the customs to be observed while dining with Attila. The cupbearers handed a silver goblet to Priscus and Maximinus. The two Romans knelt briefly in silent prayer, then each sipped from the cup, and returned it to the bearer. They were then shown to the seats they were to occupy during the feast.

Chairs were arranged along the walls of the banquet hall. In the middle of the large room sat Attila on a raised couch. Steps led to this couch which was covered with white linens and embroidered cloths. The position to the right of Attila was reserved for the person whom Attila considered the most honorable. Onegesius sat here. Facing Onegesius, still to the right of the couch, two of Attila's sons sat silently on their chairs. Attila's eldest son sat at the foot of Attila's couch, his head bent down, his eyes staring at the floor. This was his way of showing respect for his father.

On Attila's left sat the Goth Berichus. Attila had conquered the Goths, but Berichus, a nobleman, was held in high esteem by the Hun king. Also on the left, but below Berichus, sat Maximinus and Priscus. When all of the guests had been seated in the order of their rank and importance, the dining ceremony began.

A cupbearer strode proudly up to Attila and offered him an ivory inlaid wooden cup filled with wine. Attila took the cup and raised it in salute to Onegesius, the first in rank. Onegesius rose. He stood until Attila had sipped his wine and returned the cup to the waiting cupbearer. Then Onegesius drank and sat down. This ceremony was repeated individually for all those attending the banquet. Cupbearers approached the guests assigned to them. The guest rose, waited for Attila to sip from his cup, then the guest drank and returned to his seat.

When this formal salutation was over, the cupbearers went

out. Other servants immediately came in carrying tables just large enough for four men. The tables were placed in front of the seated guests, so that there would be no necessity to disturb the original order of seating.

Attila's personal servant entered, bearing raw meat on a plain wooden tray. Other servants followed, bringing more lavishly prepared food for the Romans and for other barbarians who preferred it to raw meat. Few of them did. This food was served on silver plates in sharp contrast to the tray out of which Attila dug his raw meat with his hands. The guests were served drinks in gold and silver goblets. Attila drank from a wooden mug.

Attila's clothing was as plain as his food. Other guests wore boots and swords ornamented with gold and jewels, but Attila's boots were undecorated. His sword was equally as unadorned, but it was the sword of Mars.

After the food on the first platters was consumed, the cupbearers returned. They brought goblets of wine. All of the guests stood up and remained standing until they had drunk the wine and offered a prayer or toast that Attila remain in splendid health.

Darkness came before the feast was over. When servants had cleared the tables and removed them, two barbarians entered carrying flaming pine torches. Others followed, coming up to Attila and praising him in song and verse. When they had departed, a Moorish dwarf named Zercon entered. Laughter at once filled the hall. The dwarf, with a hissing lisp, shouted words in many languages. No one could understand him. Zercon was horribly deformed, short, hump-shouldered, with huge splayfeet. His face was so flat that it seemed to have no nose, only two gaping holes in the middle of his round face. Zercon was the court jester, but Attila neither laughed nor showed any expression during Zercon's weird performance.

Priscus noted that the only expression on Attila's face came after Zercon's performance was over, when Ernach, Attila's youngest son, came up to him. Attila pinched the boy's cheeks, and the harsh expression on the king's face softened. Priscus was surprised that Attila paid no attention to his other sons, only to Ernach. A guest who spoke Latin and who was sitting beside Priscus explained Attila's affection for his youngest son. The guest first warned Priscus that he must never reveal what he was about to be told. Soothsayers and seers, according to the story, had told Attila that the Hunnish race would fall and lose its power for many years after Attila's death. The prophecies were that after a period of time, the Huns would be restored to all their power by Ernach.

The night wore on, and the drinking continued. Maximinus asked permission of Attila to retire. The king of the Huns granted the request and Maximinus and Priscus returned to their tent. The great banquet was over.

63

CHAPTER ELEVEN

Bigalas Returns

BIGALAS STAYED in Constantinople only long enough to pick up the sack containing fifty pounds of gold. Before he left to return to the Hunnish capital, Chrysaphius summoned him. The Grand Eunuch questioned Bigalas closely. What was the delay? Why was Attila still alive? Had something gone wrong with the assassination plot?

Bigalas gave Chrysaphius a detailed account of his trip to Attila's temporary camp. Chrysaphius pressed Bigalas for details of how the assassination was to be carried out.

Attila would be killed during the night while he slept, Bigalas said. Edeco would instruct the guards that Attila had stated his desire to sleep until midday. The king of the Huns was not to be disturbed for any reason. This ruse would allow the conspirators to have at least a half day's start toward Constantinople before the murder of Attila was discovered.

Bigalas radiated confidence. The more astute Chrysaphius nodded his head in agreement to the plan outlined by Bigalas. The Grand Eunuch felt that he and the Byzantine court would be the winner no matter what happened. Once Attila was dead, the Grand Eunuch cared little about what happened to Bigalas, Maximinus, or Priscus. If they were caught after the assassination, they would surely be put to death.

Bigalas left Constantinople for his return trip at about the same time that Maximinus and Priscus left the Hun capital to return to the Roman court. Many months had passed since Maximinus and Priscus had arrived at the capital. On the morning after Attila's banquet, Maximinus and Priscus went to Onegesius and asked permission to leave. Onegesius replied that Attila himself had ordered the Romans to leave. He had given this instruction after the Romans had left the banquet. Even at that moment, Attila's secretaries were preparing letters to be taken back to Emperor Theodosius.

Three days passed and Maximinus and Priscus were summoned before Attila for their formal dismissal. The Romans were honored by gifts from the king of the Huns. Berichus, who had sat above them at the banquet, was to accompany Maximinus and Priscus on the return journey.

The party left early on the fourth morning. It had traveled only half a day when a Hun in the pay of the Romans as a spy was captured by the party. The group halted, and word of the capture was sent back to Attila. The messenger returned to the group by nightfall with Attila's orders. The spy was to be impaled on a stake and left to be devoured by the birds and wild beasts.

The following day, the party was halted again when two slaves of the Huns were brought to the group. They had killed their masters during a Hunnish raid on a small village. They were caught trying to escape. Now they stood, hands bound behind their backs, before Berichus and the Hun guards in the group. This time no messenger was sent to ask Attila what was to be done with the two men. They were crucified at once, their heads severed from their bodies and placed on two tall stakes driven into the earth.

About halfway on their return to Constantinople, Maximinus and Priscus met Bigalas and his son heading westward on their way to Attila's camp. Bigalas wanted his son to see the land of the barbarians. The meeting was brief. Maximinus and Priscus noticed that Bigalas had no fugitives with him, although he had been ordered by Attila to return with all escaped Huns.

Bigalas rode on toward the Danube, the bag of gold lying across his animal-hide saddle in front of him. He pressed his horse to the limit, wishing to complete his mission as rapidly as possible. Then he could return in triumph to Constantinople with the news that the feared king of the Huns was dead.

Nightfall was approaching, and Bigalas was still some three days from the Hun capital. Suddenly, out of the dusk, a band of howling Huns swept down on Bigalas. They quickly surrounded him, dragged him from his saddle, and seized the bag of gold.

Bigalas was bound, treated roughly, and taken with his son before Attila as prisoners. Attila was not in his capital but was staying in a temporary camp. The Hunnish guards hurled Bigalas sprawling at the Hun king's feet.

Bigalas looked up in fear. Standing just behind Attila was Edeco with Orestes at his side.

Attila began to question Bigalas. Why was he carrying such a large sum of gold? Bigalas replied that it was to be used to purchase provisions for himself and his party. The gold was also to be used to purchase the release of Roman fugitives being held by Attila.

Attila listened in silence to Bigalas' hurriedly thought-up explanation for the gold. Then the Hun king spoke out angrily.

"No longer, you worthless beast," said Attila, according to Priscus' journal, "will you escape justice for your deception. Nor will there be any excuse sufficient for you to avoid punishment. Your supply of gold is far greater than necessary for your provisioning, or for horses and baggage animals to be bought for you. Or for the freeing of prisoners, which I forbade Maximinus to do when he came to me."

With this Attila ordered a guard to cut down Bigalas' son with his sword. The guard sprang on the young man and hurled him to the ground. The sharp edge of the sword was placed at his throat.

Bigalas crawled to Attila's knees. He cried out that his son was completely innocent. He pleaded with Attila to kill him, Bigalas, but to spare his son's life.

Attila ordered the guard to hold off, and Bigalas poured out the whole story of the plot. While he waited in fear for the safety of his son and his own life, Bigalas noticed that Attila and Edeco exchanged glances. Then Bigalas knew that Edeco must have told Attila of the plot when he had first returned to the Hun capital.

Attila got from Bigalas the information that he wanted. He confirmed his own suspicions that the plot had been hatched by Chrysaphius with the approval of Theodosius.

Attila ordered Bigalas placed in chains. He would not be freed until his son returned to Constantinople for another fifty pounds of gold as his ransom. The son was allowed to rise. Attila ordered Orestes to go back to Constantinople with Bigalas' son.

The gold was emptied from the bag. Attila ordered Orestes to confront Theodosius and the Grand Eunuch together. He was to appear before them with the empty bag hanging around his neck. Orestes was then to say to the Byzantine emperor: "Theodosius is the son of a nobly born father; Attila also is of noble birth, having succeeded his father Mundzuk, and he has preserved his high descent. Theodosius, since he has undertaken the payment of tribute to him, has cast out his own nobility and is his slave. Therefore, he does not act with justice toward his superior—one whom fortune has shown to be his master—because he has secretly made an attack like a miserable houseslave. And Attila will not free of blame those who have sinned against him unless Theodosius should hand over the eunuch for punishment." (This is from Priscus' journal.)

The alternative to sending Chrysaphius to Attila for

punishment was for Theodosius to behead his Grand Eunuch and send the head to Attila.

Attila never received Chrysaphius' head. Not long after the exposure of the assassination plot, Theodosius died on July 28, 450, of a fall from his horse. He was succeeded by the much stronger emperor, Marcianus. The execution of Chrysaphius was one of the new emperor's first official acts. However, the execution was not ordered because of Attila's demands. Chrysaphius had long been an evil influence in the Byzantine court, and Marcianus wanted to get rid of him.

Bigalas was later freed when his son returned to the Hun capital with the fifty pounds of gold demanded as ransom.

Attila the Hun now decided that the time had come for him to make his move toward conquest of the world.

CHAPTER TWELVE

Preparing to Strike

THE WEAKNESS of the Roman Empire of the East had been thoroughly revealed to Attila. The late Emperor Theodosius had had to resort to treachery instead of might in his attempt to overthrow the king of the Huns, and he had failed. The new emperor, Marcianus, was on the throne. The Byzantine treasury was nearly empty. Attila would see to it that it was further depleted by insisting on heavy tribute payments.

But the king of the Huns was in for a surprise.

Marcianus was no weakling as his predecessor had been. The new emperor was a Pannonian, like the great Roman general, Aëtius. He was a soldier, spirited and bold. Attila's demand for gold was met by the reply that the Byzantine Empire owed Attila nothing. His claims for gold would be met with iron. To a friendly and peaceful Attila, Marcianus would gladly make gifts. But an Attila who threatened war would be met by arms and men.

That Marcianus had little gold and even less iron in no way conditioned the new emperor's stand. Attila knew that Marcianus' reply to his demands was largely bluff, but it did cause him to change his plans.

Attila's first inclination was to attack the Roman Empire of the East. His Hunnish hordes could sweep down on Constantinople and bring Marcianus to his knees. But there was not much to gain by such a maneuver. There would be little gold to add to his war chest, and Attila still needed gold. To waste even a small part of his gold and manpower against the Byzantine Empire would not advance him far on his road to world conquest. Attila abruptly changed his plans. Rome would be his target.

The final preparations to strike at Rome began. Attila sat on his wooden throne in his wooden palace on the Danube and eagerly heard the news brought to him daily by his spies. The power of the Western Roman Empire was being chopped down through constant revolts by large and small tribes that it had held firmly under its thumb for hundreds of years. The Visigoths had seized control of all of Aquitania, which later became the Provence of Guienne of medieval France. The Vandals ruled Africa and threatened the Italian coasts. The Alans, a large tribe which had migrated east from the Caucasus a hundred years before, controlled the banks of the Loire River and were wavering in their allegiance to Rome. Rome's hold on Gaul was endangered by the Bagaudae, a large body of insurrectionist peasants who roamed the forests of what is now France, striking at Roman legions and towns governed by the Romans.

Emperor Valentinian III was seriously worried. His spies brought back reports of the Huns' daily preparations for war. Large tribes of Asiatic Huns were answering Attila's call to arms. Valentinian's own mercenaries were complaining about being underpaid.

Was the fall of the Roman Empire at hand? It seemed so, as evil omens appeared daily and panic spread among the Roman people. Statues were said to have tears falling from their eyes. Loud claps of thunder in a clear sky were interpreted as the clashing of weapons in the heavens. The earth trembled and, on one occasion, the people of Rome cried out that a rain of blood was falling from the sky.

Valentinian consulted with his soothsayers. He was told that all these weird omens were connected with the ferocious Huns.

In Attila's capital, the king of the Huns was also consulting with his soothsayers. The future was read from the entrails of chickens, from the foam of boiling water. Priests and sorcerers wailed and danced to the gods of war. Attila's palace was littered with statues of the gods worshiped by the peoples he ruled. The palace was in a constant uproar as these gods were called upon to reveal Attila's destiny.

Soothsayer consulted sorcerer. Asiatic magi consulted Buddhist monk. They gathered before Attila and proclaimed their prophecies. The king of the Huns would become the lord of the universe. Attila would conquer all.

The signs were favorable. The Hun capital bulged with fierce warriors. Weapons were sharpened, bows restrung. The attack was ready to begin. But Attila's first move was not with the sword. He called for the casket containing the ring sent to him by Honoria fifteen years before. Again he changed his plans.

The ring and a letter were sent by swift messenger to Valentinian. In the letter, Attila stated that he was now ready to accept the hand of Valentinian's sister, offered to him by Honoria herself in her proposal of marriage.

Attila extended an invitation to the whole imperial family to attend the wedding. He reproved Valentinian for having had his sister confined for so many years. She must be released at once to become the bride of the king of the Huns. Attila added quite casually that he expected to receive as Honoria's dowry the property to which she had been entitled on the death of her father—half of the Western Empire.

Attila had no romantic interest in the Roman princess; he already had over three hundred wives. To get just another wife meant nothing to him; but a wife who would bring to him half of the Western Roman Empire was certainly worthy of being added to his harem.

When Valentinian received Attila's letter, he flew into a rage. True, his sister had acted disgracefully, but no matter what her conduct had been in the past, no act of Honoria's could be as disgraceful, as repulsive, as marriage to the king of the Huns.

Valentinian consulted with his First General, Aëtius, upon whom he had been leaning more and more heavily as the war clouds gathered. Aëtius' reply in no way lessened Valentinian's fury. Aëtius pointed to the ring. Honoria had pledged herself to Attila—the ring was evidence, Aëtius said. But there was one way out—marry Honoria off immediately. Valentinian quickly took this suggestion.

Honoria was hurriedly removed from the convent where she had been held a virtual prisoner for so long and was married at once to the man to whom she had been promised fifteen years before, Herculanus, now an old man and still a loyal supporter of the Roman court.

Aëtius then advised Valentinian to send a reply to Attila explaining the situation. Regretfully, Valentinian would not be able to grant the request of the king of the Huns. Honoria was already married.

Valentinian also took care to point out that under Roman law the empire belonged to the males of the ruling family, not to the females. Honoria, therefore, was not entitled to any of the property of the Roman Empire.

It is highly doubtful that Attila ever believed that he would gain half of the Roman Empire as a dowry. He was much too shrewd to place his hopes on such a ruse.

The time had come. Attila made a hurried inspection of his armies. He summoned his strongest allies, Ardaric, king of the Gepidae, and Theodemir, king of the Ostrogoths. Each would command a major force in support of Attila's attacking Huns.

As the year 451 began, Attila was ready. His massed armies of over half a million fierce tribesmen were eager for battle. The king of the Huns, with the sword of Mars at his side, rode out of the Hunnish capital on the first leg of his great adventure—the conquest of the world. His howling Huns swarmed behind him.

CHAPTER THIRTEEN

The Scourge of God

REPORTS POURED IN daily to Valentinian's court in Rome. Never had there been such a vast buildup of men and arms as was seen in the Hun capital on the Danube. The Huns were on the march.

Aëtius worked frantically. The great Roman general rallied his allies. He called on the Franks in Gaul. The Franks were scattered Teutonic tribes that roamed in areas of the middle and lower Rhine River. Aëtius called on the Saxons, the Burgundians, the Visigoths, and the Alans still loyal to Rome. He strengthened Roman cities and reinforced the fortresses.

The great historian Edward Gibbon wrote: "The nations from the Volga to the Atlantic were assembled."

Attila's plan was to strike first against the Franks and the Visigoths. He showed his military genius by this move. Attila had arranged a treaty with Genseric, king of the Vandals, for the Vandals to raid the Italian coasts. This move would prevent the Romans from coming to the aid of the Franks and the Visigoths. Attila would conquer them, enslave them in his armies, and turn them—as his soldiers— against Rome. The lands of the Franks and Visigoths were rich in grazing area and ripe for plunder. The terrain was well suited to the methods of war long practiced by the Hun horsemen. Attila also wanted to strengthen his relations with Genseric. The Visigoths were growing into a strong nation in the southern provinces of Gaul and were looking hungrily across the Mediterranean Sea at the Vandal kingdom.

The ground trembled as the vast throng of horsemen and chariots moved out of the capital. Wild cries and shouted songs rose above the rumble of the chariots and the thudding of horses' feet. Yellow-skinned, fur-clad Mongols, with Attila riding in the fore, took the lead. Their deadly lassos looped in the air. Ostrogoths, wearing leather garments and carrying long lances and battle-axes, followed. Giant Germans, their yellow hair flowing in the wind, came next. They were followed by a second wave of barbaric Huns, recently arrived from Asia.

It was a wild, terrifying army that Attila led. A thousand different dialects were spoken by the bloodthirsty troops. But although the army was weird-looking and wild-acting, it was disciplined. Attila's command was firm. The savage barbarians were held together by their complete confidence in their leader and by their fired-up zest for war. Thoughts of plunder and of the spoils that went to the victor raced through their minds.

Attila's army swept westward toward the Rhine Valley with unbelievable speed. Town after town fell to his conquering force. The Burgundians offered no resistance. The Franks along the Neckar River, a tributary of the lower Rhine, were vanquished in a single, lightning strike. Their king, a vassal of Rome, was murdered. Attila proclaimed a new king who rode by his side as the Huns neared the Rhine.

It had all been so simple, so easy. Chariots were piled high with the loot taken by the conquering Huns. The peoples of the regions overrun by the Huns offered no resistance. They were terrified by these barbarians. There had been little fighting, only a few skirmishes. The Roman garrisons in the small villages, certain of defeat, withdrew before the approach of the Hunnsh hordes.

At the banks of the Rhine, Attila called a halt. His victories had been so easy that he feared a trap. Aëtius and the Roman legions might be lying in ambush across the rolling waters of the Rhine. Attila also wanted to rest his troops, and to allow the supply chariots to catch up with the faster-moving horsemen.

Everywhere he went, in every village that fell to his might, Attila proclaimed himself as the friend and savior of the inhabitants. His true enemy was Rome, he said. He would bring about the downfall of the Roman Empire which had held these villages in near slavery for so many hundreds of years.

While waiting for the rear guard of chariots to arrive, the

men hurriedly put together pontoon bridges and stretched them across the Rhine. Attila and his hordes crossed the river near Koblenz. Their headlong onrush was checked for a day or two when a large number of Burgundians surprisingly offered the first real resistance that Attila had met. Led by their king, Gundicar, and joined by a roving tribe of Franks, the enemies met in the Rhineland just north of Worms. The battle was fierce but short-lived. The Huns crushed the Burgundians and Franks, captured Childeric, king of the Franks, and destroyed the city of Worms.

The army of more than half a million roared down the western bank of the Rhine, laying waste to the countryside and razing every town and village in their path. Attila deployed his troops in a wide wave stretching westward from the Rhine across what is now the northern border of France. He crossed into northern Gaul and hurried his troops at the fortified city of Metz.

Metz was well garrisoned. The walled city had plenty of provisions, and it was governed by a bishop who had once been a warrior of note. The bishop refused Attila's demand to open the city's gates.

The Huns, invincible when fighting on open plains, had little experience in taking a fortified walled city. Only a few thousand had been part of the seizure and destruction of the fortified city of Naissus. Now frantic Huns tried to scale the walls. Battering rams were brought into action and pounded on the city's gates. The Hunnish arrows bounced off the city's walls.

Metz put up a stubborn fight. Boiling oil and flaming pitch were poured down on the heads of the besiegers. Huge stones were heaved over the walls to knock horsemen off their steeds. Many horses, crippled from the force of the rolling stones, had to be destroyed.

Attila became more and more furious as Metz refused to fall to his forces. No city, no people, no tribe had checked his onrushing armies thus far. Attila, wise as a warrior, knew that the delay at Metz could well break the rhythm of his advance and dishearten his plunder-hungry troops. He decided to raise the siege and march westward toward Reims.

So the king of the Huns abandoned Metz. But after one day's march, he called a halt. As a skilled general, Attila knew well the danger of leaving a strong, undefeated enemy in his rear, so he sent his scouts back to check. When they returned, they confirmed Attila's theory. The inhabitants of Metz had laid down their arms and were making repairs in the city. Quickly Attila reversed his army. On April 7, 451, the Huns swept back to Metz and in a few hours massacred the city's inhabitants, including the bishop and other churchmen—all who had defied him.

Word of the massacre spread throughout northern Gaul. The people of Reims trembled as the Huns approached, and many fled the city. Nicaise, the Bishop of Reims, rallied a few brave men, but their defense lasted only a few hours. Nicaise was murdered; the brave men who had fought with him were slain. Thus, Reims fell.

A monk who had heard of the death of the Bishop of Metz and who witnessed the slaying of Nicaise, labeled Attila "the Scourge of God." It was a title in which Attila took pride. He valued highly his reputation for fierceness. He saw to it that word was spread around, about the persons he had tortured, crucified, or impaled. He did this purposely to inspire greater fear in his enemies and make his conquests less difficult.

With the fall of Reims, Attila moved his army farther westward, easily capturing and sacking the villages of St.-Quentin and Laon, then called Laudunum. On the road to the south lay the large town inhabited by the Lutetians—the town that was later to become Paris. People poured into the city daily, bringing with them tales of horror, of villages burned, of people put to the sword. The Lutetians had sworn an oath of loyalty to Rome, and now Rome's greatest enemy was on the way to their town.

All of northern Gaul had fallen to the king of the Huns. Attila rested his troops for a few days, preparing to move against the Lutetians—but their city was saved by a sudden change in Attila's plans. Spies planted in the Visigoth court at Toulouse, in southern Gaul (now France), learned that King Theodoric I was being pressured by Roman envoys to join his armies with Aëtius in order to defeat the dreaded Hun. When the spies brought this news to Attila, he decided to bypass the Lutetian city and move swiftly to the south of Gaul where he would crush Theodoric and the Visigoths before they could be joined by Aëtius' Roman legions.

Attila planned to cross the Loire River at Orléans. This region was inhabited by the Alans, whose leader, Sangiban, was wavering in his loyalty to Rome. Attila sent luxurious presents to Sangiban and a huge bribe with the ultimatum that Sangiban and the Alans could accept the friendship of the Huns or be driven from the Loire Valley. Sangiban accepted Attila's terms and sent word back to the king of the

Huns that the bridges over the Loire at Orléans would be open to the Hun army.

Early in May, A.D. 451, five months after his army had moved out of the Hunnish capital on the Danube, Attila arrived under the walls of Orléans. His all-conquering troops had covered nearly one thousand miles, laying waste to hundreds of towns and villages in their path.

Orléans, destroyed by Julius Caesar four hundred years before, had been rebuilt into a strong, heavily fortified, and well-guarded city, governed by Bishop Aignan, who was loyal to Rome and distrustful of the Alans.

The gates of Orléans were closed as the Huns thundered across the Loire bridges and took up siege positions under the city's walls. Attila, his army increased by the addition of Sangiban's Alans, felt that Orléans would fall readily to his avalanche of soldiers.

Bishop Aignan dispatched couriers to Aëtius in Rome and to Theodoric in Toulouse. He must have help at once or the Huns would sweep all of Gaul. Theodoric, fearing the Huns would overrun Toulouse and march into Spain (and the Visigoth empire), also sought aid from Aëtius. Although Theodoric distrusted Rome, he distrusted Attila even more.

Weeks passed as the Huns laid siege to the walls of Orléans. Aignan had slipped out of the city and hastened to Toulouse, where he urged Theodoric to come to his aid. Theodoric promised that he would come to the rescue within fifteen days. He was waiting only for Aëtius and the Roman legions.

The Bishop of Orléans returned to his embattled city, and told of the promise of rescue. Guards were doubled all along

83

the walls. Tar and oil pots were kept boiling constantly. Each charge of the Huns was repulsed. Once again the army of the Huns was showing its greatest weakness. Although the city of less than fifty thousand people was surrounded by a fierce army of well over half a million, the Huns' attacks were thrown back time and time again. As the days passed slowly, Orléans' defenses began to weaken. The staunch defenders could not hold out much longer. The people of Orléans were beginning to doubt their governor, the Bishop of Aignan. Where were Theodoric and Aëtius?

Toward the end of June, nearly seven weeks after the Huns' first attack on Orléans, a section of the city's walls tumbled. Attila's troops poured in, burning and pillaging. In the southern part of the city, the defenders were engaged in hand-to-hand combat with the Huns. Suddenly, atop the southern wall, a great shout rose from the guards. A cloud of dust told of the rapid approach of a large army. It was the Roman legions, led by the great General Aëtius. Theodoric I, king of the Visigoths, rode by his side.

Attila had no desire to meet his enemies in the confines of a walled city and he sounded a retreat. The Huns' pillaging was abruptly halted as Attila ordered them out of Orléans.

Aëtius and Theodoric pressed Attila hard. They struck at the rear defenders of Attila's army and inflicted severe losses. According to the historian Gibbon: "The valor of Attila was always guided by his prudence." The king of the Huns made a quick survey of his position. What he saw he did not like. He ordered his generals to reorganize their troops. Attila would retreat. He did not consider this a defeat, but he wanted to draw his enemy onto a terrain more suited to the fighting methods of his barbarian army. Instead, he would make his stand on the Catalaunian Plains surrounding Châlons on the Marne River. (This was probably southwest of the present city of Châlons-sur-Marne.)

The Battle of Châlons in June, 451, was to become one of the most decisive battles in world history.

CHAPTER FOURTEEN

The Battle of Châlons

THE NIGHT BEFORE the great battle, the Franks, led by their king, Mérovée (Merovaeus), met with the Gepidae, Attila's allies. In this brief preliminary skirmish, fought under the light of burning torches, fifteen thousand warriors were slain.

At dawn reports of the short but bloody conflict were brought to Attila. Of those slain, two-thirds had been Gepidae warriors. It was a bad start for the king of the Huns, but more bad news was to follow. When Attila had set up his camp, he had not noticed a hill to the right of his center. Since it was above Attila's camp, this hill, if held by the enemy, would give the opposition an outstanding advantage. Young Torismond, prince of the Visigoths, was storming that hill even as Attila was conferring with his generals.

Attila dispatched a strong force to repulse Torismond's attempt to take the hill, but the Huns were thrown back. Torismond and his Visigoths held on.

Attila's anxiety increased. In the first two engagements with the enemy, the Huns and their allies had met defeat. Attila delayed before sounding the battle call which would bring the two great adversaries into open conflict. First he would consult his *haruspices,* diviners who could predict the future. The bodies of several enemy victims were brought before Attila's tent. They were cut open, and the haruspices read their entrails. Next, the fortune-tellers scraped the bones of the victims, and from these two examinations, chanted out their prophecies. The signs pointed to the defeat of the Huns, disheartening news to Attila, who had already suffered two defeats. The sorcerers continued their chanting. They saw also the death of Attila's adversary. To Attila, this could only mean Aëtius, the Roman general. The Hun leader brushed aside the prediction of his own defeat, rejoicing in the prophesied death of his greatest enemy.

A fog rolled across the Catalaunian Plains, blanketing and blotting out the more than a million warriors waiting for battle. Attila mounted his horse, pulled the sword of Mars from its scabbard, and rode among his troops. He sensed the dejected spirits of his men, who had been shaken by the two early defeats. Rumors of the haruspices' predictions were already sweeping the camp.

Attila knew that he must raise the spirits of his warriors. He must rebuild the fires of fierce savagery that had made them invincible until now. So he spoke of the past glory of the Huns. He spoke with the strong voice of a king and a conqueror. The Romans would be trampled under the feet of the Hunnish horsemen. The Visigoths would be destroyed. He was the Scourge of God. He wielded the sword of Mars.

"I myself," Attila said, according to the historian Gibbon, "will throw the first javelin, and the wretch who refuses to imitate his sovereign is doomed to inevitable death."

The spirits of the barbarians rose by the example and the confident voice of their leader. The troops shouted their impatience for the battle to begin. Attila had brought his men to the fever pitch which he desired in them. He immediately formed his order of battle.

The king of the Huns deployed his forces westward from the bank of the Marne River. Attila placed himself at the head of his brave and loyal Huns, directly in the center of the long line of warriors. On his right flank, Attila placed Ardaric and his Gepidae. On his left flank, the Ostrogoths were in position, led by three brothers—Walamir, Theodemir, and Widimir. Directly behind Attila were his camp and baggage, ringed by chariots.

The array of the opposing armies placed Theodoric and the Visigoths opposite their kindred tribesmen, the Ostrogoths. Aëtius and his Roman legions confronted Ardaric. Attila's opposing force were the Alans, led by Sangiban, who had been Attila's ally in the siege of Orléans.

Aëtius and Theodoric had purposely placed Sangiban in the center of their stretched-out line. Both distrusted the

89

faithless king of the Alans, and they suspected treachery on his part. Placed in the center, Sangiban could be closely observed.

Prince Torismond and his division of Visigoths still held the hill. They were positioned directly behind Ardaric's Gepidae. Although Torismond's force was not large, it overlooked Attila's armies from the rear, and the arrows it rained down on the Hunnish forces did exceptional damage. Attila was actually in a poor position, for the enemy was both in front and in the rear of his troops.

The fog covering the Catalaunian Plains lifted after midday, and in the ninth hour of the day (3 P.M.) the battle was joined. Attila dashed toward the Roman line, and hurled his javelin to signal the start of the great conflict. He turned, raced back to his Huns, and moments later the sky was darkened as arrows from the opposing armies filled the air. The flight of arrows was brief. When all had been expended, the cavalry charged.

Attila led the charge. The king of the Huns wheeled and turned, dashing among his horsemen, urging them forward. Sangiban's Alans met the Hunnish charge head on. There was a clash of spears bouncing off metal shields. The Alans wavered and were forced back. Attila, now triumphant, shouted a command. The Hun king led his horsemen to the left to join the Ostrogoths, who were being severely punished by Theodoric's forces. Hunnish infantry rushed into the gap left by Attila's horsemen and met the Alans in hand-to-hand combat.

Theodoric rallied his horsemen to meet the additional challenge of Attila's charge. He rode among his men, shouting encouragement, inspiring them to even greater efforts against the enemy. A javelin flew through the air from the hand of Andages, an Ostrogoth. Its aim was true. It pierced Theodoric's chest and he fell from his horse. In the furious fighting, Theodoric's own horsemen rode over their king, trampling him to death.

Shock at the death of their king spread quickly throughout the ranks of the Visigoths. They were thrown into confusion without their leader. As they began to panic and flee, down from the hill dashed Prince Torismond. Now the Visigoths fought with renewed fury. They turned and charged the Ostrogoths and Attila's supporting cavalry. Attila and the Ostrogoths were forced to yield. They fell back slowly to the center where the Hun horsemen had made the first charge. On came the Visigoths, wheeling on the flank of the Hunnish infantry, still furiously engaged with the faltering Alans.

Aëtius and his Roman legions had charged Ardaric and the Gepidae and had cut them off, isolating them between the Marne and the hill held by Torismond's Visigoths. The Roman general, feeling that the fate of the West, and the Roman Empire, were at stake in this battle, aroused his Roman and Frankish soldiers to their greatest efforts and was slashing his way to victory.

Attila, still fighting at the head of his Huns, was slowly being forced back. The Visigoths were pressing him from the left flank; Aëtius and the Roman legions had turned on his right flank. Attila was being pinned down from both sides. The Alans, supported now by the pressure from both sides, struck back at the Hunnish infantry. Attila was in a pocket. His only escape was to the rear. He was forced to retreat.

Night was falling as the battle ended. Attila retreated within the circle of chariots surrounding his camp. Archers manned the chariots and drove off the repeated charges of the opposing forces.

Attila, fearing total defeat, swore that he would never be taken alive. He ordered wooden saddles to be removed from the horses. These were piled into a high funeral pyre. At the base of the pyre were piled all the spoils and loot that the Huns had captured in the westward drive. If the enemy broke through the circle of chariots, Attila would mount to the top of the funeral pyre. As the enemy approached, the Hun would signal for the pyre to be lighted. He would die in the roar of flames before allowing the enemy to take him prisoner. However, Attila did not have to use his hastily made funeral pyre.

A silence suddenly descended over the Catalaunian Plains as night drew its dark curtain over the field of one of the bloodiest battles ever fought. Attila, king of the Huns, the Scourge of God, had been defeated. The last great battle between the barbarians and the West was over. The West was victorious. Had Attila and his Huns prevailed, the entire course of history might have been changed. Christianity might have been wiped out, and Western civilization, tracing its beginnings back to Greece, might have been destroyed and barbaric rule taken its place.

The Battle of Châlons has been included as one of the fifteen decisive battles of world history by Sir Edward Creasy. Creasy, a nineteenth-century British historian, compiled his selections in 1851, begining with the Battle of Marathon and ending with the Battle of Waterloo. This was, of course, long before the two devastating world wars in the twentieth century. Before World War I, no single battle in history had taken as many lives as the Battle of Châlons. Estimates range as high as 300,000 killed in the fierce fighting that lasted only about six hours. It is recorded that the river Marne ran red with blood from the thousands slain along its shores. More recent historians think it doubtful that the death toll was as high as recorded by ancient chronicles. But there is little doubt that the number of warriors slain on both sides was enormous.

From Damascius, an ancient Syrian philosopher, comes the story believed for many years after the battle, that the fighting was so fierce that "no one survived except only the leaders on either side and a few followers: but the ghosts of those who fell continued the struggle for three whole days and nights as violently as if they had been alive; the clash of their arms was clearly audible."

Dawn on the day following the battle revealed the terrible carnage that had taken place. Bodies of slain warriors and carcasses of dead horses lay strewn upon the field of battle as far as the eye could see. Little of the earth showed through the blanket of the dead.

The Battle of Châlons was over, but the opposing armies remained in position. Attila had been defeated, as predicted by the haruspices. The sorcerers had been right in their second prediction, too. Theodoric, king of the Visigoths, had been killed. He was one of Attila's greatest enemies. But when Attila learned that it had been Theodoric, not Aëtius, who had fallen, he went into a violent rage.

Aëtius, in the camp of the victors, took a quick, estimated count of those slain. It could not be an accurate one, but there was no doubt that the greater losses had been suffered by Attila's armies.

The Visigoths immediately proclaimed Prince Torismond their new king to succeed his father Theodoric. Young Torismond, his spirits high with victory, wanted to press on, to destroy completely the forces of Attila.

Aëtius, however, urged caution. He stressed to Torismond the fact that Attila was still dangerous. "Would it not be foolhardy," Aëtius asked, "to risk the victory so recently won?" However, this was not Aëtius' real reason. The Roman general feared the Visigoths, and Torismond's troops far outnumbered those of Aëtius. If Attila fell under a second attack, Torismond, already bold and proud, might well turn on Aëtius. The Visigoth empire was already strong and growing stronger. It presented a definite threat to the rule of Rome.

Aëtius, with the fate of Rome always foremost in his thoughts, played on Torismond's thirst for power. He pointed out to him that in the Visigoth court at Toulouse, Torismond's four brothers, Frideric, Turic, Rotemen, and Himmerit, might well want to seize the throne, even though Torismond had been proclaimed the new king.

This argument swayed the young leader, and by late afternoon, the Visigoth army under its new king gathered up its arms, struck its tents, and marched south toward Toulouse.

Aëtius had still another reason for not wanting the total destruction of Attila and the Huns. In the past, the Huns had been Roman mercenaries, and the barbarians had filled the ranks of the Roman legions. With the Visigoth empire now a definite threat, the day might soon come when Aëtius would have to call on Attila and his Huns to fight with the Roman legions. Chastened by his defeat, Attila might well become an ally of Rome, or so Aëtius reasoned.

But Aëtius was wrong. Attila still hated the Romans, and his hatred was even greater now that he had been defeated by the Roman general. Attila wanted the defeat of Rome, and he still planned to take Honoria for his bride.

With the Visigoths gone, Aëtius assembled his army, and the victorious Roman legions turned their steps toward Italy.

Attila remained at Châlons for another three days. He suspected a trap with the sudden withdrawal of the Romans and the Visigoths. When no new maneuver developed, the king of the Huns rallied his defeated armies behind him and started to retrace his path back to the Danube.

Attila had been defeated, but he was by no means through. Once again Rome was to feel the might of the Hun king, for Rome itself was the next target decided upon by the Scourge of God.

CHAPTER FIFTEEN

A Man of God

As ATTILA LED his weary, defeated army on the long journey back to the Danube, he was pursued across the Rhine, deep into Germany, by Mérovée and his Franks. The Franks made continuous raids on Attila's rear guard, harassing the Huns and killing many of them. At night the Franks kindled numerous small fires, many more than they needed, to give Attila the impression that he was being pursued by an extremely large force. The strategy worked. Attila did not turn on his tormentors. Had he done so, the smaller Frankish army and its leader would undoubtedly have been wiped out by the superior Hunnish forces.

Mérovée followed Attila until he reached Thuringia in central Germany; then the Franks turned back to the Rhineland. The Thuringians were allies of Attila; they had joined him on his westward march, and had fought for him at Châlons. On their way back to their homeland, Attila and the Thuringians took many Franks as hostages and captives, among them two hundred young maidens. In Thuringia, the hostages and captives were massacred. The fate of the two hundred young maidens is described by the historian Gibbon: "The two hundred young maidens were tortured with exquisite and unrelenting rage; their bodies were torn asunder by wild horses, or their bones were crushed under the weight of rolling wagons; and their unburied limbs were abandoned on the public roads as a prey to dogs and vultures."

On reaching the Hun capital on the Danube, Attila established winter quarters, holding his still large army under his command. The failure of Attila's expedition into Gaul seemed in no way to impair his reputation as a leader. The hundreds of tribes of barbarians remained loyal to the king of the Huns. The large army rested throughout the winter, and with the coming of spring their spirits rose. They were ready to march again, to follow their leader Attila at his first command.

Throughout the winter months, Attila plotted his next move. It would be against Rome. In the spring of 452, he sent messengers to the court at Rome, repeating his demand for Honoria and for half the Roman Empire which Attila insisted was rightfully hers. Again the demands were indignantly rejected.

Attila sounded the call to arms. His well-rested troops responded with high spirits, eager to be on the march again. The king of the Huns led his host of barbarians over the Carnic Alps and down the western slopes of the Venetian Alps into northwestern Italy. His passage over the Alps, clear of snow with the approach of summer, was swift. The Huns would strike first against the strongly fortified city of Aquileia. At this period in history, Aquileia was one of the richest, most populous, and strongest of the maritime cities on the Adriatic coast.

During the winter months back in the Danube capital of the Huns, Attila had had many engines of war and battering rams constructed. He even had his troops trained in the battle tactics of the Roman legions. He remembered Metz and Orléans, and his troops were drilled in the art of the siege.

Aquileia was the northwestern gateway to all of Italy. The city had to be captured to allow Attila free movement to the south and to Rome.

But once again, Attila's troops proved to be ineffective against a well-fortified city. Attila hurled his engines of war against the walls. Catapults threw stones weighing as much as three hundred pounds against the heavy timbers surrounding the city. Bronze-tipped battering rams crashed against the gates without letup. Attila had his carpenters build tall, movable towers on wheels. These were rolled up to the walls so that the archers could be more effective in firing at the defenders. But still the city held out.

The siege continued for three months, but the city did not weaken. Provisions were running low in Attila's army. The meat ration was cut to once a week. Scavenger troops scoured the rich countryside for chickens, geese, cattle, horses—anything that would feed the hungry army. Murmurs of rebellion began to rise among the warriors. The barbarians did not like this type of warfare. They had been too long accustomed to the sweeping charge of the cavalry on open plains. They exulted in rapid movement, in sudden clashes with the enemy. The long siege was wearisome and dispiriting.

On the other hand, Aquileia was well provisioned and there was plenty of water inside the walls.

After the three long months of siege, Attila believed that the city was impregnable. His troops were becoming more rebellious, so the Hun king issued an order to cease fire and the attack was halted. In the morning, the troops were to strike their tents and prepare to retreat to the Danube.

Italy might have been spared and Attila once more defeated had it not been for the actions of a bird. The king of the Huns had become more and more superstitious as he grew older. In his march from the Danube to Italy, he had, on several occasions, spared churches and cathedrals in the towns he razed, believing that he heard the voices of the Christian God warning him away.

Now, as he prepared to end his invasion of Italy that afternoon, Attila rode around the walls of Aquileia. He was in an angry mood. Edeco, his faithful warrior, rode by his side. Suddenly, the king of the Huns reined in his horse and looked at one of the watchtowers raised above the high walls of the city. Attila pointed to a large bird, a stork. As the two warriors watched, the stork flew from its nest. This,

100

indeed, was a good omen. In an excited, cheerful voice, Attila told Edeco that a stork, so closely identified with human beings, would never leave its nest unless it knew that the destruction of the walls which supported the tower was imminent. The superstitious king said that animals, especially birds, had a keener sense of future happenings than men had. This was the greatest of omens.

In high spirits, Attila once more rallied his armies. He ordered them to prepare for an all-out assault at dawn the following morning. A blast of trumpets signaled the beginning of the attack. The Huns, angry and resentful at the sudden change in plans, attacked the walled city with renewed fury and an increased vigor which had been lacking in their assaults of recent weeks.

Ladders were hurled against the walls. The seige towers were rolled up and archers swarmed to their tops. Battering rams pounded with crashing thuds. Finally a breach was made in the wall. Angered and infuriated Huns poured through the gap. From the towers, archers took deadly aim and the staunch defenders of Aquileia were cut down. The city was ravaged, its men, women, and children massacred.

Attila rode among the dead and dying. He granted his maddened troops two hours to pillage. Then he ordered the city put to the torch. According to Gibbon: "The succeeding generation could scarcely discover the ruins of Aquileia." The city never recovered its former greatness, and even today, it is a small village of about fourteen hundred people.

The Huns, maddened by their victory, dashed westward.

Milan and the Pavia and Torino provinces fell before their onslaught. The Italian people, who had not seen enemy troops on their soil for forty years, everywhere surrendered without battle to the advancing Huns.

In Milan, Attila took over the royal palace, and flew into a rage when he saw a huge painting. It depicted the Caesars seated on their throne and the barbarian princes and chieftains prostrate at their feet. Attila commanded a painter to reverse the figures. He had himself placed on the throne, and the Roman emperors on their knees at his feet.

The official Roman court at this time was in the city of Ravenna on the Adriatic Sea. When Aquileia fell, Emperor Valentinian III fled Ravenna and hastened to Rome. His action was foolhardy, for Ravenna was a fortress city and Rome was open. But Valentinian fled, despite the pleas and advice of the great General Aëtius. Aëtius had rallied the Roman legions and was prepared to make a stand against the onrushing Huns. But Aëtius was in disgrace. He had been severely criticized by Valentinian and Marcianus, the Roman emperor of the East, for not completely destroying Attila and the Huns at Châlons. He had little support from the Roman court, and he demonstrated his greatness as a man as well as a general by remaining loyal to the Roman Empire, despite the disdain with which he was treated by high officials of the court.

In Rome, the weak Valentinian announced his intention to flee to Gaul at the approach of Attila the Hun. He was dissuaded from doing this by ambitious court officials, who led him to believe that that was just what Aëtius wanted him to do. With Valentinian in Gaul, they pointed out, Aëtius would be free to take over completely and establish himself as the Roman emperor. Valentinian hesitated, and in desperation pleaded with Pope Leo I to meet with Attila.

The historic meeting took place on the banks of the Mincio River, where it flows into Lake Garda near Verona. Pope Leo, an impressive figure in flowing white robes and surrounded by members of the clergy dressed in gold and silver, filled Attila with awe. It is not known what was said between the Scourge of God and the man of God, but Attila listened long and respectfully to the words spoken to him by the Pope. It is recorded that during their long conversation, the apparitions of St. Peter and St. Paul, the patron saints of Rome, appeared. They are said to have menaced Attila with instant death if he failed to heed the plea of their successor, Pope Leo. (A painting by the great Italian artist Raphael depicts this meeting.)

Attila's mind was assaulted by imaginary fears. His superstitions and his awe of the Christian God caused him to listen to the eloquence of Leo with respectful attention. Attila granted the Pope's plea that he give up his intention of capturing Rome. He also may have been influenced by the fact that plague and hunger threatened his armies. Gibbon records that Attila was promised an immense dowry belonging to Honoria, and that later he would have her as his bride. For Pope Leo's work in the deliverance of Italy and Rome from the savage barbarian, he gained the appellation of *Great* to his name.

Before Attila ordered his troops to go home to their capital on the Danube, he swore that he would return and bring about even greater destruction to Italy if his promised bride, Princess Honoria, was not sent to his ambassadors within the time limit that was set.

Proud, having brought Italy to his heels, Attila once more turned his horse toward his own capital. He was now about forty-seven years old and he was never again to ride against the Roman Empire.

CHAPTER SIXTEEN

A Broken Bow

SONGS OF VICTORY rose over the blare of trumpets as Attila led his triumphant army back into the Hun capital in the year 453. He was greeted by graceful maidens under their white banners of silks and linens.

Quickly the word spread about the capital that the king of the Huns had brought with him a beautiful young Burgundian princess called Ildico, who was to become another of his many wives. The wedding ceremony and Attila's triumph in Italy were to be celebrated with all barbaric pomp and festivity in the sprawling wooden palace of the king.

Chariots bedecked with wild flowers came rumbling into the Hun capital, bearing princes and chieftains of Attila's vassals. Gifts of gold, jewels, finely woven fabrics and rugs, embroidered silks, and gold-decorated saddles were brought to the wooden palace.

Throughout the day of the wedding, the fields around the palace rang with the clashing of weapons and the shouts of daring horsemen as they played at games of war. Buffoons, clowns, and court jesters vied with one another to entertain the crowds thronging about the palace.

As nightfall approached, the great wedding banquet commenced. The beautiful Ildico, a transparent veil covering her face, sat beside her husband, her eyes lowered, shyly acknowledging the compliments of the many guests. Attila matched drink for drink with the princes and chieftains who toasted his great success and his newest marriage. Attila's wooden goblet was filled with wine time and time again. The feasting and drinking lasted far into the night.

That same night in Constantinople, Marcianus, the Roman emperor of the East, startled his retainers by suddenly crying out in his sleep. Court officers rushed to his bedside. Marcianus told them of a dream that he had had. He had seen Attila in his dream, bow in hand, its bowstring stretched, as the king of the Huns prepared to fire the deadly shaft. Suddenly, the bow snapped, cleanly broken in two. An augury, proclaimed Marcianus, an omen that a great enemy of the Byzantine Empire was dead.

In the Hun capital, Attila and his young bride retired shortly after midnight. The drinking and feasting continued into the early hours of the morning. The next day the guests

106

slept late, exhausted by the extravagance of their long hours of festivities.

At noon, Attila still had not appeared. At first this caused no particular concern. But as the day drew longer, Attila's closest friends and advisers began to worry. The loyal Edeco went to the king's room. He knocked on the door, softly at first. Receiving no reply, he knocked louder, pounding on the door. Edeco shouted his master's name. No reply answered his shouts.

Edeco burst open the door and cried out in horror. He saw Attila lying unclothed upon his great bed. Its white fur coverlet was stained with blood. Edeco rushed to his master's side. Attila the Hun was dead. Ildico sat by the bedside, tears running down her cheeks, trembling with fear.

At first Attila's friends and ministers thought that their king had been assassinated, but examination of the body showed no wounds of any kind. Attila had died a natural death. During his heavy, alcoholic sleep, an artery had burst. He had hemorrhaged heavily; a torrent of blood had flooded into his lungs.

The king of the Huns' body was carried to the plain nearest his palace and displayed under a silken pavilion. All that day and throughout the night, chariots wheeled around the pavilion as princes and warriors and chieftains chanted out funeral songs in memory of their hero.

Attila's body was placed in three caskets. The first was made of iron. This casket was encased in a casket of silver and, in turn, the silver and iron caskets were placed into a casket of gold. Prisoners were brought to dig the grave. It was a large grave and into it were placed the spoils of many nations. The triple casket of gold, silver, and iron was lowered into the grave and covered. The gravediggers were killed so that enemies would never know the exact location of Attila's final resting-place.

Hunnish warriors tore out their hair and slashed their faces so that their king would be mourned not in tears but in blood as befitted so great a leader.

This was the end of the Hun empire. Attila's many sons tried to carry on, but tribal chieftains who had been loyal to Attila, gave none of this loyalty to the sons. Nor was the prophecy ever fulfilled that Attila's son Ernach would one day restore the Hun empire to its full power and glory. The hundreds of Hunnish tribes scattered all across Europe and Asia. As the years passed on, the Huns were absorbed by other nations.

Attila's reign had been long and, for him, glorious. He was the most powerful ruler in the world for a score of years, from A.D. 433 to 453. Of this man, called the Scourge of God, Priscus, the historian, wrote:

"He was a man born to shake the races of the world, a terror to all lands, who in some way or other frightened everyone by the dread report noised abroad about him, for he was haughty in his carriage, casting his eyes about him on all sides so that the proud man's power was to be seen in the very movements of his body. A lover of war, he was personally restrained in action, most impressive in counsel, gracious to suppliants, and generous to those to whom he had once given his trust."

Robert N. Webb's interest in the men who have helped to shape the course of world history goes back to his reportorial days on newspapers in New England and New York City. "Whether the events shape the man or the man shapes the events," says Robert Webb, "knowing about the key men of the world in their special time is vital to the new generation's understanding of its own role today." Mr. Webb's writing sphere is wide, but for several years he has focused in both his fictional and factual works on those who have left their marks on the pages of history. Here, in *Attila: King of the Huns,* he brings the reader the life of one of history's most feared and hated men.

Mr. Webb has been a reporter, an editor of periodicals in the United States and in South America, and a public relations director, but has devoted his recent years to full time authorship of books for the young adult reader. He is married and has two children who share their father's interest in the cinemascope of the world.

Index

INDEX

113